THE
COMMUNITY KITCHENS
COMPLETE GUIDE
TO

SIMON AND SCHUSTER · NEW YORK

Gourmet Coffee

JOHN De MERS

Copyright © 1986 by Community Kitchens
All rights reserved
including the right of reproduction
in whole or in part in any form
Published by Simon and Schuster
A Division of Simon & Schuster, Inc.
Simon & Schuster Building
Rockefeller Center
1230 Avenue of the Americas
New York, New York 10020
SIMON AND SCHUSTER and colophon
are registered trademarks of Simon & Schuster, Inc.
Designed by Edith Fowler
Manufactured in the United States of America

10 9 8 7 6 5 4 3 2 1

Library of Congress Cataloging-in-Publication Data

DeMers, John, date–
  The Community Kitchens complete guide to
gourmet coffee.

  Bibliography: p.
  Includes index.
  1. Coffee. 2. Cookery (Coffee) 3. Cookery.
I. Title.
TX817.C6D46 1986   641.3'373   85-26197
ISBN: 0-671-55870-6

Illustrations on pages 39, 50, 56, 60, 89, 91, 118,
129, 130, 133, 171, 181 and 198 are from the New
York Public Library Picture Collection.

To Sandra,
Sara and Michael

Acknowledgment

Community Kitchens would like to acknowledge the work being done by the Coffee Development Group to create a better understanding of the merits of quality coffee.

Contents

Introduction

*U*NTIL recently, most people did not contemplate much more than the day ahead as they sipped their morning cups of coffee. However, America's favorite beverage—that taken-for-granted dark brew—has suddenly become an experience of concern, complicated and sophisticated. And beyond the pleasures and subtleties that each cup releases lies a challenge.

Each step required to achieve that cup of coffee has become incredibly more complicated but also vastly more interesting. Who would have ever guessed that the process would involve more than picking a can or jar from the grocery shelf without breaking stride? Yet, Americans have been discovering other sources for coffee in record numbers. Perhaps 3 percent of the coffee drinkers have deserted their grocery brands for the new world of gourmet coffees. Another 15 percent use gourmet coffees for special occasions. These coffees generally must be acquired at specialty coffee or food shops, or the gourmet coffee or food sections of the more upscale grocery stores or by home delivery through mail or phone order. This select group of coffee drinkers has discovered that coffee

9

can be much different and much more than they ever expected. For them, price is no longer the criterion for the selection of their coffee. They happily pay two or three—and occasionally ten—times what they would pay for their now-abandoned grocery brand. However, the change did not stop at the grocery shelf. The majority of these gourmet coffee drinkers purchase coffee in whole bean, which, in fine coffee, means they also have to acquire a coffee grinder. The investment does not end with this $20 to $200 purchase: many consumers also throw out their percolators or old automatic drip pots and acquire new coffeemakers at a cost of $75 to $300. Some even keep an assortment—one for every day, a small one, one for travel, an espresso machine, and perhaps a manual drip or French drip for sentimentality and special taste.

Suddenly, it is understood that coffee offers all the subtleties of origin that wine offers and more. Unlike wine, however, one brews one's own coffee. The gourmet coffee drinker aspires to become a coffee master. This book is a condensation of information that we at Community Kitchens have been disseminating to coffee lovers for more than three generations, answers to questions they asked and some they should have asked.

For us, the gourmet coffee market is the latest development in three generations as coffee specialists. It all started with Cap, my grandfather, in his neighborhood grocery store in 1918 in Baton Rouge, Louisiana. Our story could not have happened outside of South Louisiana. The Cajun and Creole cultures of South Louisiana had never abandoned their European appreciation for dark roasted coffees. And we never lowered our coffee standards to accept the watery brew of the rest of the country. The Saurages also hold the belief that there is only one way to do anything, the right way. Cap, as a grocery store owner, was dissatisfied with many of his products, but most of all, the coffee available in Baton Rouge. Therefore, he had his own coffee blend roasted especially for him in New Orleans. With this step, the future of the Saurage family and the coffee drinkers of South Louisiana was irreversibly altered.

Cap did not envision providing the country or the world

with his coffee. His special coffee was for his friends and customers and named, appropriately, "Community." But when his brother-in-law needed work, Cap provided him a truck and sent him on the road to sell coffee to other Baton Rouge grocers. By 1924, the coffee business was bigger than the grocery business, and the store was closed so Cap could concentrate on coffee. As each generation entered the business, they expanded the availability of Cap's coffee. Cap's sons, Norman, Jr., and Cary, opened branches in Lake Charles and Houma, Louisiana. When Cap's grandchildren, Roland, Cary and Linda, entered the business, they opened the catalog and mail order division, which now serves customers across the country.

Each generation also brought improvements, as Cap did by having coffee roasted to his specifications. Norman, Jr., purchased a roaster in order that Community could select and roast its own green coffees. Then came better roasters and packaging. The grandchildren continued this standard of using new coffee processing and packaging equipment to provide a greater variety and the finest quality products available.

With this book, the Saurage family shares all it knows and has become with all coffee lovers as we do with our millions of customers.

—ROLAND SAURAGE

The Light History
of a Dark Brew

SINCE the true enjoyment of coffee has always been tied to its romance, several intriguing tales have taken on importance—even if they've never taken on reality.

There is no specific mention of coffee in the ancient writings of the Greeks or Hebrews, but there is a minority chorus that seeks to translate the drink from famous literary works. Some, for example, find coffee in Homer, insisting that the *nepenthe* Helen brought with her out of Egypt was nothing more exotic than coffee mixed with wine. And others conclude that the "black broth" of the Lacedaemonians was closely akin to the coffee drunk around the world today. Finally, some scholars go to great lengths to find coffee in the Bible—perhaps as the five measures of parched corn given by Abigail to David in hopes of appeasing his wrath, or as the red pottage for which Esau sold his birthright, or as the parched grain Boaz ordered be given to Ruth.

However, for all the western fetish for finding coffee's origins in its classic books, nearly all evidence points to discovery a bit farther east and considerably later in history. Yet even here the record gets cloudy, with two of the most persistent legends surrounding the evolution from bean to beverage. One concerns a certain Sheik Omar, who had been exiled from Mocha in 1258 for some unspecified moral failing. Facing starvation and finding nothing but berries around him, he fell upon these, boiled them in a saucepan and drank the thick brew they produced. It so happened that Omar was a physician as well as a priest, so that when some of his patients sought him out and tasted his new medicinal drink, they carried his praise back to Mocha. The governor himself then invited Omar to return, even building him his own monastery.

The other major legend surrounding coffee's discovery spotlights Kaldi, a herdsman in upper Egypt or Abyssinia who noticed that his goats became unusually lively after feeding on berries that grew nearby. The animals, said one version, "were abandoning themselves to the most extravagant prancing." Kaldi, over time, decided this was too much pleasure for goats to keep to themselves, so he too took to munching on the beans. It was the abbot of an adjacent monastery who observed Kaldi's exhilaration and experimented with boiling the coffee beans. He and his followers found that the drink they produced encouraged them to pray.

Apart from these colorful yarns, passed down from the Arabs in translations by French explorers, it is believed that the coffee plant is native to Abyssinia and probably to ancient Arabia. Its first cultivation is recorded in the year 575, when a Persian invasion ended the Ethiopian rule of a *negus* known as Caleb. Despite its early start, however, the spread of coffee was quite sluggish until the fifteenth and sixteenth centuries—a fact some historians attribute to the Arabs' attempt to control its commerce. Realizing perhaps just what they had, these savvy merchants blocked all transport of green coffee beans; only boiled or parched beans, which could not germinate, were exported. The Arabs thereby maintained their hold on the marketplace.

Coffee Spreads Out

These Moslem businessmen eventually were thwarted by an aspect of their own religion, the pilgrimage to Mecca. The coffeehouses of the Near East, spread with rugs, peppered with poets and serving each patron up to twenty cups a day, were simply too spectacular to remain a monopoly forever. Berries inevitably slipped out among the thousands of pilgrims, proving that at least a few had more than Allah on their minds. As early as 1600, in fact, an Indian named Baba Budan returned home and planted coffee seeds near his hut in the mountains of Mysore. Most of the plants cultivated today by the people of Coorg and Mysore appear to be descendants of these.

About the time Baba Budan was gardening around his hut, word of coffee was spreading west as well, thanks to botanists from Germany, Italy and the Netherlands who visited the sultry Levant. The Dutch were the first to get excited about trade, transporting a coffee plant from Mocha to Holland in 1616 and beginning serious cultivation in Ceylon in 1658. The Dutch were responsible for introducing coffee to Java (establishing a basis for the drink's most famous nickname). The burgomaster of Amsterdam joined forces with the commander of Kananur in Malabar to grow plants from the seeds of *Coffea arabica*. These initial attempts were knocked out by an earthquake and a flood, but fresh cuttings were shipped in three years later to start the line of all coffees grown in the Netherlands Indies.

From Bontekoe's Drey Neue Tractatgen, *1688*

Wishing to show off their success in the East, the Dutch brought back their first coffee samples in 1706 and set them up for admiration in the botanical gardens of Amsterdam. Plants begun from seeds produced there were distributed to some of the better-known gardens and conservatories all over Europe as a testimonial to the Dutch empire, which extended at the time to Sumatra, the Celebes, Timor, Bali and many other islands.

The French, spurred by dreams of riches and wounded national pride, decided quickly they would not be out-done. Yet an early attempt to imitate the Dutch in Dijon was such a disaster that the town's name was destined instead to be associated with mustard. Seeds brought in from Amsterdam stubbornly resisted cultivation in Paris, until the French government talked the Dutch into send-ing a healthy five-foot plant to Louis XIV's château in Marly in 1714. This was transferred with great pomp the following day to Paris's Jardin des Plantes. The pomp, it seems, was well deserved, for this single plant became the progenitor of most coffees grown in the French col-onies, along with those of Mexico, Central and South America.

- DE CLIEU AND THE NEW WORLD

Drawn to Paris by personal affairs from his military posting in Martinique, Gabriel Mathieu de Clieu con-ceived the idea of taking back some coffee plants. De-pending on which story you believe, he succeeded in gaining permission at court through the aid of the royal physician or through the aid of a lady to whom the physi-cian could not say no. It is further unclear whether or not de Clieu's first coffee plants perished during the long voy-age to the Caribbean, but it is certain that by 1723 coffee was growing in Martinique. As the captain himself tells the tale, he transported his precious seedlings in a box covered with glass to absorb and retain the rays of the sun, fended off pirates and wild storms, even shared his personal water ration with the plants when the ship found itself becalmed.

The plants took to Martinique with gusto and repro-duced rapidly at de Clieu's estate at Prêcheur. The first

harvest was gathered in 1726; de Clieu felt compelled to surround his plants with thorn bushes and even armed guards to keep others on the island from sharing the wealth. The captain gathered a batch of seeds weighing about two pounds and passed them out to those he thought "most capable of giving the plants the care necessary to their prosperity," setting the stage for nature to take a hand.

The year after de Clieu's historic harvest, an earthquake with a flood at its heels wiped out all the cocoa trees on which the island's people survived. The cocoa plantations were immediately turned over to coffee and produced enough healthy plants to share with Santo Domingo, Guadeloupe and other adjacent islands.

Island Hopping and Beyond

De Clieu's miracle on Martinique was repeated similarly in Haiti and Santo Domingo. The tiny island called Réunion did so well at coffee cultivation under the French Company of the Indies that it was able to enter the export arena in less than a single decade.

As the French had once looked to the Dutch, the Dutch and others soon looked to the French. The first coffee in Brazil began with plants from French Guiana, though later a coffee tree from Goa in Portuguese India made it to Rio de Janeiro with even greater acclaim. A Belgian monk named Molke, fired by paeans to Rio's soil and climate, presented some seeds to the Capuchin monastery there in 1774. Later still, a bishop named Joachim Bruno took up the cause and encouraged cultivation not only in Rio but in Minas, Espírito Santo and São Paulo.

The English, meanwhile, took coffee to Jamaica; the Spanish from Java to the Philippines. Santo Domingo transported seeds to Cuba by 1748, and by the waning days of the century coffee was growing in Guatemala, Puerto Rico, Costa Rica, Venezuela and Mexico.

Though the natural conditions were extraordinary in the Caribbean and Latin America, this was by no means the far frontier of the coffee explosion. Seeds from Rio were used to begin planting in Hawaii in 1825. Fifty years later the British began propagation in central Africa, though it took them another quarter century to extend the business to their colonies in East Africa. Thanks to the French, coffee growing got its start in Tonkin, in what then was Indochina, in 1887. And a small but successful industry grew up in Queensland, Australia, beginning in 1896. Obviously, someone out there was drinking plenty of coffee.

A Quick Cup in the Piazza

Venetians today point with pride to the wonders of their city, even though most of them were commandeered for their maritime empire in raids along the eastern Mediterranean. Through conquest, the Venetians became great acquisitors, and one of the best things they ever acquired was coffee. News of the drink that would for centuries draw tourists to the Piazza San Marco first hit town in 1580, via a physician and botanist who had visited Egypt. "The Arabians and the Egyptians," wrote Prospero Alpini, "make a sort of decoction of it, which they drink instead of wine; and it is sold in all their public houses, as wine is with us." Alpini's references to medicinal qualities attributed to coffee found their way into the literature of European doctors, even though his offhand comparison of coffee to wine had a more immediate impact.

Coffee could not have found a more powerful promoter in Catholic Italy than Pope Clement VIII. According to at least one story, some Italians saw in the beverage's heathen roots a threat to their very souls—not to mention their wine sales. So they appealed to the Pope to have this invention of Satan forbidden to Christian palates. The devil, they argued, had substituted this hellish black brew after prohibiting his Moslem followers the wine so essential to Christian sacraments.

This broadside stressed that if you "this Rare Arabian cordial Use, then thou may'st all the Doctors' shops refuse," 1674.

The Pope decided to taste coffee for himself and found its aroma and taste so much to his liking that he not only refused to ban the drink, but gave it instead his official blessing. "Why, this Satan's drink is so delicious that it would be a pity to let the infidels have exclusive use of it," he said. "We shall fool Satan by baptizing it, and making it a truly Christian beverage."

With this strong push from high places, coffee quickly grew from a medicine sold at apothecary shops to a beverage with a setting it would come to call its own—the coffeehouse. After three or four decades of sale by strolling lemonade vendors, the first such establishment in the West was opened in Venice in 1683, less than fifty years before the still-popular Caffè Florian opened its doors on St. Mark's Square. The double "f" was a holdover from the word *Coffea*, but little else from antiquity survived. The rush to open coffeehouses along the square had begun. Before long, hanging around the piazza, sipping coffee and badmouthing the government had become a tradition observed closely by radicals, anarchists, artists and poets well into the twentieth century.

Perhaps sensing the trouble ahead, the Venetian government tried to clamp down early. When it heard that a group of radicals had proposed a reading room at the Caffè della Spaderia to encourage the spread of their ideas, the rulers sent a soldier to drag the first person entering that room before their tribunal for justice. The radicals abandoned their proposal rather quickly. On another occasion, the so-called Inquisitors of State sought to eradicate coffeehouses completely, branding them "social cankers" given to immorality, vice and corruption. Yet the Venetian caffè not only survived but spread to Rome, Florence and Genoa.

These gathering places became colorful social experiments attracting coffee drinkers from all classes, even if they tended to gather at different times of the day. Mornings were usually given over to working men, while in afternoons and evenings coffeehouses were the domain of the leisure class. The chosen beverage of these people even found itself promoted in a literary and philosophical journal published for a time in the 1760s. It was called *Il*

Caffè, after the setting in which the publisher and his friends discussed issues of the day. The journal folded after just two years, but the drink and the socializing it celebrated had entered Europe to stay.

A Thoroughly French Affair

The passionate romance that today deposits coffee drinkers along the Champs Elysées and in squares throughout the City of Light actually got its start in the provinces. As it had in Venice a few years before, coffee arrived in France by sea. Several merchants from Marseilles who had spent much of their time in the Levant decided to come home, bringing with them a supply of their treasured beans. Later, merchants and druggists joined forces to import the first coffee in bales from Egypt, with entrepreneurs in Lyons following suit. The drink caught on so quickly and physicians became so alarmed that they forgot where the practice originated, fearing it "would not agree with the inhabitants of a country hot and extremely dry."

France saw a threat in coffee consumption similar to that perceived and presented under the guise of religion in Rome—yet true to the French character, the trappings of this threat were far more secular. The French launched a medical attack on coffee, but the controversy that erupted in Marseilles had as much to do with wounded pride and fiscal self-service as legitimate concern about public health.

In 1679, the town's good doctors strong-armed a young student into arguing before the faculty of Aix that coffee had surpassed wine in popularity everywhere it had been introduced, even though it was unfit to fill even the lowliest of French carafes. The student blasted the beverage as a foreign perversion. It was not really a remedy for anything, he said, because it was not a bean at all but the fruit of a tree discovered by camels and goats. And it burned up the blood, causing palsies, leanness and, worst of all, impotence. The faculty agreed wholeheartedly, but the world had turned a few too many times to buy into

Cartoon of a Parisian coffee seller, 1695

such a transparent libel. If anything, consumption of coffee gained fresh momentum in France from its new status as forbidden fruit. "None," wrote the French writer La-Roque, "from the meanest citizens to the persons of highest quality, failed to use it every morning or at least soon after dinner, it being the custom likewise to offer it in all visits."

Ever the victim of fashion, Paris took to drinking coffee with the same passion it now reserves for the rise or fall of a hemline. The craze was kicked off by a Turkish ambassador—one Suleiman Aga by name—who arrived in the capital in 1669 to serve at the court of Louis XIV. Fortified against the posting far from home, he carried with him great mountains of coffee beans and embarked on a pattern of lavish entertaining that set all Paris to talking. Coffee—thick, black, sweetened with sugar and served with great ceremony—was the star of these soirées.

Like small-time versions of the Aga himself, immigrants from the East were creating a market for coffee in the very streets of the city. An Armenian named Pascal, brought to Paris by the ambassador, sold coffee from a tent at the Fair of St. Germain. The drink itself came complete with service, including boys peddling it to the crowd from tiny cups on trays. After the fair, Pascal

At the St.-Germain Fair: A set for a play

opened a coffeeshop near the Pont Neuf. He quickly learned here, however, the market was for beer, so he sent his boys back out into the streets shouting "Café! Café!" from door to door. When even this approach failed, Pascal packed up his beans and went off to friendlier territory in London.

In spite of its quick popularity in some quarters, the French in general seem to have at first resisted coffee, apparently due to its association with Oriental settings, as well as with immigrants from coffee-drinking lands. Indeed, most French gentlemen would have turned up their noses at this foreign brew and its exotic presentation. It was only when French entrepreneurs became involved, setting up spacious apartments with tapestries, mirrors and chandeliers, that drinking coffee outgrew the privacy of small soirées and took on the badge of Parisian respectability.

Cafés eventually figured prominently in two of France's most memorable social activities: revolution and bohemianism. It was in the middle of the Café Foy in 1789 that a young journalist named Camille Desmoulins worked himself into such a frenzy of oratory that he and his followers marched out to overthrow the government. The Bastille fell just two days later. In the 1800s, the cafés Momus and Rotonde found themselves at the center of an artistic and literary movement that kept the Latin Quarter jumping through the "Lost Generation" of the 1920s until the American Depression went global a decade later. A number of coffeehouses closed, but the institution—and the tradition—survived hard times.

By this time, of course, Parisian cafés were far more than coffeehouses. They were places to see and be seen, to wallow in a floodtide of alcohol, to denounce a mistress or a husband. Most of all, perhaps, they were places to avoid the dreaded empty canvas or blank sheet of paper. They were nonetheless places that confirmed for all time the status of coffee at the heart of Parisian social life.

Soldiers, Spies and Strudels

Few coffee tales can match those from Austria and Germany for color, intrigue or sheer bombast. The beverage's entry into Vienna, for example, involved 300,000 Turkish soldiers, a spy with a flair for business and nothing less than the fate of all Europe.

Mohammed IV sent his men out from Constantinople in 1683, and nothing less than conquering the continent would do. The troops quickly surrounded Vienna—ever a vulnerable outpost in the European East—and cut it off from the rest of the world. Unfortunately for Vienna, it was also cut off from friendly armies under the Duke of Lorraine and good King John of Poland. The fall of the city would mean Europe would be under the Turks; and a future enlarged by Strauss waltzes and Freudian analysis would have been doubtful.

Because of the terrible military situation, a spy was sought who could move through Turkish lines. One Franz George Kolschitzky stepped forward, a native of Poland who had lived in the East for years and knew the language and customs. Wearing a properly ornate Turkish uniform, Kolschitzky made his way through the enemy lines not once but several times, providing a communications link that enabled the friendly armies to send the Turks back where they came from. The fleeing soldiers left on the outskirts of Vienna 25,000 tents, 10,000 oxen, 5,000 camels, a large quantity of gold—and several Alps' worth of coffee beans. The Viennese, seeing no use for the last, tossed them into the bonfires—until Kolschitzky caught a whiff from his past.

Scrambling, the hero of Vienna's darkest hour saved the beans from the flames and wrangled the right to cart them away, along with a charter to open the city's first coffeehouse. His establishment, under the sign of the Blue Bottle, operated successfully for many years and spawned an official guild of others similarly engaged; they were, simply, *Kaffe-sieder* or coffee makers.

The coffeehouses that followed the Blue Bottle's lead were lively places indeed. The institution, it seems, appealed to the Viennese constitution that favored hard work broken at regular intervals by cake and conversation. The *Kipfel*, a pastry defiantly baked in the shape of the crescent of the Turkish flag, paired nicely with the beverage discovered under siege. *Krapfel*, a pastry commissioned by Kolschitzky himself, was also married to coffee from the start. Today these are called doughnuts. Hands not holding *Kipfel* or *Krapfel* were generally turning newspapers or gesturing wildly in debate. The freedom with which the Viennese expressed themselves was a shock to visitors from other, less fortunate corners of the continent. "They speak without reverence," wrote one early tourist, "not only of the doings of generals and ministers of state, but also mix themselves in the life of the kaiser himself."

Thanks to Kolschitzky's espionage, Germany was spared its own showdown with the Turks. But the Germans had embraced the infidel's favorite drink years before the threat. Germany, in fact, provided the first European literary reference to coffee in reports from Aleppo by Leonhard Rauwolf. The first coffee came via London, initially to Hamburg but later as far east and inland as Berlin. Englishmen operated nearly all early cafés, which were known as English coffeehouses. By the mid-1700s, during the reign of Frederick the Great, there were at least a dozen coffeehouses in Berlin proper, with many more tents serving coffee in the suburbs.

Again, however, native commerce took offense at the foreign intrusion. Coffee found its way not only into coffeeshops but into German households as well, supplanting beer as the most popular refreshment. This greatly annoyed Frederick the Great, who embarked on one of the most tangled prohibition campaigns in history. First, he engineered a campaign by German physicians that closely resembled the earlier one in France. Coffee, said the doctors, caused sterility in men and infertility in women.

Next, Frederick tried to use his licensing power to limit coffee to the aristocracy—a strange move indeed considering the sterility scare. "His majesty was brought up on beer," insisted Frederick the Great, "and so were his ancestors, and his officers. Many battles have been fought

Richter's coffee house in Leipzig, about 1750

and won by soldiers nourished on beer; and the king does not believe that coffee-drinking soldiers can be depended upon." He even employed retired military men to sleuth through the streets sniffing for bootleg beans roasting in some clandestine kitchen. Coffee became a status symbol for the wealthy and the poor fell back not on beer but on a host of coffee substitutes—barley, wheat, corn, chicory, even dried figs. As a last-ditch effort at making his mandate stick, Frederick concocted a bizarre manifesto that noted with disgust the amount of money pouring out of the country via the coffee trade.

Beer made a brief resurgence under Frederick's heavy hand, but coffee in time returned to its former preeminence—mostly on the strength of purchases by a new breed of German *Hausfrau*. No longer in the fields working beside her husband, she adopted coffee as the perfect beverage for sessions of relaxation and gossip while her good burgher was away at his desk. The nervous husbands, for their part, branded this chatter as *Kaffeklatsch*, a name that eventually came to convey the get-togethers themselves. In retrospect these gatherings seem a declaration of independence for German womanhood. After all, neither Frederick the Great nor their husbands had been able to stifle their free talk or free thought.

A Golden Age in England

English readers got their first inklings of what coffee was all about in 1601, courtesy of yet another miraculous marriage of samaritanism with self-interest. In that year, a Briton named Anthony Sherley sailed from Venice to Persia on what was at best a self-appointed diplomatic mission. Little can be said of the trip's impact on international relations, yet it had quite an impact on the history of coffee, since one member of the party recorded his impressions of the "damned infidels." Once again, the Turks' favorite drink was central to the report: "They sit at their meat (which is served to them on the ground) as tailors sit upon their stalls, crosse-legged; for the most part, passing the day in banqueting and carowsing, untill they surfet, drinking a certain liquor, which they do call coffe."

The first cup of coffee brewed in England was almost certainly drunk by Conopios, a native of Crete who had served under Cyrill, the religious patriarch of Constantinople. When his boss was strangled by the vizier, Conopios wisely fled to England, where he caught the eye of observers with the beverage he prepared each morning. Just over a decade later, the first English coffeehouse was opened in Oxford by a native of Lebanon who christened his establishment "At the Angel in the Parish of St. Peter in the East," no small mouthful in itself. Students from all corners of the British Isles enjoyed the drink so much they soon founded the Oxford Coffee Club, forerunner of the Royal Society.

London's colorful coffeehouses can serve as a window on what Isaac D'Israeli called "the manners, morals and the politics of the people." The British Museum acknowledges this fact with its displays of coffee para-

The "Bourse" in Lloyd's Coffee-house, about 1798

phernalia, including the first advertisement for the beverage, a handbill distributed in 1652. "The Vertue of the COFFEE Drink First publiquely made and sold in England, by Pasqua Rosee . . . in St. Michael's Alley in Cornhill . . . at the Signe of his own Head." The first newspaper ad, appearing five years later in the *Publick Adviser* of London, claimed the drink "closes the Orifice of the Stomack, fortifies the Heat within, helpeth Digestion, quickneth the Spirits, maketh the Heart lightsom, is good against Eye-sores, Coughs, or Colds, Rhumes, Consumptions, Head-ach, Dropsie, Gout, Scurvy, Kings Evil and many others."

Clearly, there was a place in English society for the coffeehouse. Before its appearance, men of all interests and means had been forced to seek pleasure in the country's taverns—great places for drinking and singing but not very conducive to the sprightly exchange of ideas. The popularity of coffeehouses, in fact, proved so dramatic that the keepers of Britain's alehouses launched a propaganda campaign that finally convinced Charles II to issue an order seeking the suppression of coffeehouses. Public

During the Great Frost of 1683–84 Londoners carried on their activities on the frozen Thames, which included visiting Duke's Coffee House (number 2, front row, far left).

outcry, however, resulted in an extremely short life for the mandate. It was issued on December 29, 1675, but retracted January 8—two days before it was to take effect.

Unlike the bawdy taverns of the day, the coffeehouses of London were renowned as far away as the continent for their strict standards of behavior. Conversation inside was so energetic yet so wrapped in propriety that the establishments earned a nickname that stuck, "penny universities." At that price, admission to a world of impressive thought was opened to many who could not afford Oxford or Cambridge. By the time England stepped into the eighteenth century, London boasted as many as 2,000 coffeehouses. Before long, every profession, trade or class had its favorite coffeehouse, one that evolved an atmosphere to reflect its clientele. Group became clique, and clique became club, eventually demanding a house of its own away from the public coffee bar.

The history of London coffeehouses is a litany of fa-

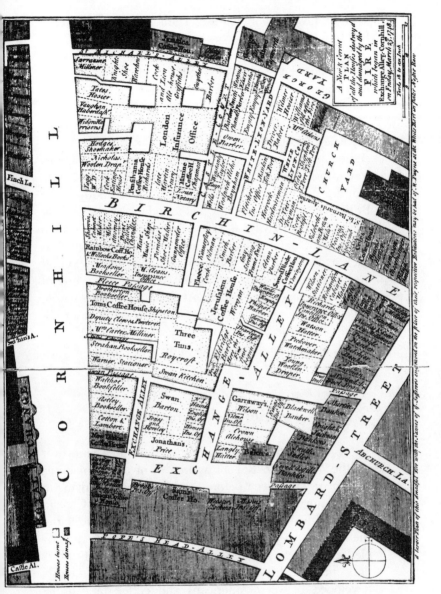

This map of London as it was before the fire of 1748 gives some idea of the number of coffee houses in existence.

mous names—St. James's, Will's, Garraway's, White's, Slaughter's, The Grecian, Button's, Lloyd's, Tom's and Don Saltero's. An early periodical called the *Guardian* received its mail at Button's, while the *Tatler* and *Spectator* grew out of conversations between Addison and Steele at their favored coffeehouse. Daniel Defoe and Henry Fielding turned up to work over the literary fashions of the day. Later, Samuel Johnson teamed up with actor David Garrick to form a club at the Turk's Head, one that over time counted several generations of notable writers and thespians among its members.

Despite the luminaries who gathered there, however, the English coffeehouse began to fade by the close of the eighteenth century. For one thing, coffee had made its way into households as a breakfast and dinner beverage, diluting its market in public settings. For another, the British East India Company had found itself better able to cultivate tea, making it argue that nothing else should serve as the national drink. And finally, exquisite gardens such as Ranelagh and Vauxhall had begun to siphon off customers, serving women as well as men—and a host of beverages as well as coffee. At first, these places were called pleasure gardens, a name they no doubt deserved. Yet in time the afternoon choice of most women prevailed, and tea gardens they became.

Beverage of Choice for Rebels, Pioneers and Immigrants

As far as anyone can tell, no coffee came over on the *Mayflower*. But an awareness of coffee made its way to America even before the Pilgrims did, arriving in the memory and perhaps the pantry as well of Captain John Smith. When Smith made landfall in 1607 to found the colony of Virginia at Jamestown, he had already traveled extensively in Turkey and tasted extensively of its dark, bracing drink. The close relationship that quickly developed between Americans and coffee fanned the flames of revolution and fortified the rebels against the challenges they would eventually face.

The first written reference to coffee in America turned up in 1668, when a beverage brewed from roasted beans and sweetened with sugar, honey or cinnamon was served in New York. Two years later, the drink made its way to New England, and coffeehouses on the English model were soon set up in every one of the colonies. New York, Boston and Philadelphia boasted of some of the oldest and finest, yet the establishments also took on social importance in Norfolk, Chicago, St. Louis and New Orleans.

Coffeehouses like the King's Arms, the Merchants and the Exchange did double duty in old New York, since their premises sometimes were used for assembly meetings and even for criminal trials. Similarly, in Boston they served as headquarters for a small but growing army of firebrands tired of George III's tyranny; then the most famous houses included the King's Head, the Indian Queen and the Sun in Faneuil Hall Square, but the city's most significant was beyond doubt the Green Dragon. Located on Union Street, at the heart of the town's commercial center, it figured in virtually every political and social event in Boston for 135 years. In Boston, John Adams and Paul Revere plotted with their compatriots at the Green Dragon.

In the 1800s, coffee headed west with the settlers, joining teas made from garden herbs, spicewood and sassafras root as a favored beverage of the trail. According to legend, the site of Fort Laramie, Wyoming, was traded by Indians for tools, weapons, riding gear and several sacks of brown roasted Javas. The American Army included green coffee beans in regular rations during the Mexican War; these the soldiers roasted over campfires and prepared, once they'd picked up the trick, in the Latin *cafe con leche* style. During the Civil War, Union soldiers were issued 100 pounds of food and either 10 pounds of green coffee beans or 8 pounds of ground roasted coffee. To show no favor, each portion was spread out evenly and distributed by a sergeant who turned his back while calling out the men's names.

The very expansion that made America powerful made it a nation of coffee drinkers as well. In Spanish Florida, the drink had long been familiar through close ties with Spanish Cuba, a preference that did not abate with statehood. The mammoth Louisiana Purchase delivered to the Union not only New Orleans but a ribbon of coffee-loving French towns along the Mississippi River. The great European immigrations of the late 1800s brought still more coffee drinkers to the fresh, developing continent.

The Industrial Revolution brought traumatic change to the young country, but America's love of coffee was part of the culture. In fact, the drink took on added importance as a refreshment and stimulant for workers putting in sixteen-hour days.

Coffee, Creoles and Cajuns

Creoles loved their coffee with a passion unique in their still-young nation. The children of French and Spanish colonists, Creoles were the most affluent and flamboyant of Louisiana's early residents. The first opera in the country was their relaxation, politics their daily bread, and coffee the beverage that got most Creoles on their feet in the morning and kept them going through work and play.

"*Noir comme le diable*," a Creole invariably responded when asked how he liked his coffee. "*Forte comme la mort. Doux comme l'amour. Et chaud comme l'enfer.*" The phrase itself evokes the role coffee played as one of life's elemental forces, the power that somehow helped the world have meaning. Black as the devil. Strong as death. Sweet as love. And hot as hell. When asked the best way to produce such a brew, a Creole invariably trotted out the way he always made his.

As late as the twentieth century, there were Creole men in New Orleans who never thrust a foot from their beds before downing a first cup of strong, sweet coffee. Creole wives enjoyed no such luxury, even on the chilliest mornings, but children, wandering in from their own warm beds, were sometimes treated to a sip or two. It was a taste few youngsters forgot. For most, it was the start of a life-long appreciation that blended fine taste with even finer memories.

Once things were hopping around the Creole homestead, it was time for *café au lait*. This silken combination was prepared with attention to detail worthy of a religious ceremony—and the Creoles were as religious as their love of pleasure permitted. Hot coffee and scalded milk were poured into the cup at precisely the same moment, swirling up a rich bubbling brown that sent aromas throughout the house and even into the street. To stroll down a Creole street in the morning was to become a coffee lover for life.

Though taste served to vary the food served at breakfast, there was one choice that not only verged on universality but a kind of sanctity as well. Crisp doughnuts called beignets were fried up in oil so hot they puffed out in surprise, filling with air in a way that became their trademark. These light wonders were then buried in powdered sugar and devoured in astonishing numbers with cup after cup of café au lait. It's no surprise that for all the Creole customs that have faded, there are still sidewalk cafés that pour coffee and milk at precisely the same moment, that still serve beignets fresh from the kitchen and sugary blizzard white.

Though the Cajuns joined the Creoles in Catholic faith and French heritage, the similarities tended to end there. It was hard to pry a Creole away from New Orleans, with all its culture and its commerce. Yet many Cajuns happily and purposely lived and died without ever seeing the city. Cajuns generally avoided cities and their stifling rules of behavior. Life was better on the bayou, with wonderful food developed from unlikely ingredients—and plenty of strong black coffee.

In the mid-1700s, the fortunes of war had sent the Cajuns scurrying down the Eastern Seaboard from their home in Nova Scotia. What had been French was suddenly English, and terribly uncomfortable. A few of the exiles, separated from loved ones and herded onto ships, found welcome along the route south, creating pockets of Thibodeaux and Fontenots from Maine to Georgia. But nearly all met resistance until they found a place absolutely no one felt like fighting for—the flat, mosquito-infested marshland along the murky Gulf of Mexico. With little initial enthusiasm but even less choice, the Cajuns set about turning puddles into paradise.

They felled cypress trees for homes, furniture and churches, and they cleared the land and planted it. Drawing on ideals set down by their ancestors, they built large families in which men hunted, farmed and fished while women cooked from dawn till dusk. And from things only Indians had ever dared taste—alligator, nutria, crawfish —they fashioned a cuisine that would be hailed two centuries later as the greatest America had yet produced.

Before long, in fact, the Cajuns came to believe they had stumbled on the nation's best-kept secret, a land that rewarded their labors with immeasurable sensory delight. Seen from a sunset-pink veranda in southwest Louisiana, Nova Scotia seemed rocky, frigid and infertile. The Cajuns had found a home.

The cuisine they perfected looked back to sixteenth-century France, to the hearty fare of the countryside. Yet its reliance on the freshest ingredients—and the coincidental unavailability of almost any other kind—made it quickly take on an appearance and taste dramatically its own. Along the sandy shores of the gulf, Cajuns learned to celebrate seafood from shrimp to oysters to fish, while inland Cajuns mastered the careful preparation of game. Their culture's love of hunting produced more than philosophical satisfaction or masculine bravado; it supplied each kitchen with a year-round parade of versatile waterfowl and fresh red meat.

These joined the homegrown wonders of the Cajun farm—chicken, pork, beef and a wild array of vegetables —as the basis of a spicy, ever-various cuisine. Indeed, the foods Cajuns cooked proved so irresistible that the Creoles of New Orleans incorporated many touches into their finest restaurant dishes.

From farm to bayou fishing camp, the Cajuns reveled day and night in strong black coffee, preferring their brew without Creole chicory but every bit as bracing. They usually drank their coffee black and sweetened in the pot, with a flavor and feel surprisingly similar to that found in the eastern Mediterranean. The beverage was generally enjoyed from a demitasse, with some Cajuns not encountering full-sized cups until business took them away from home.

In the remotest sections of Cajun country, a trip to buy coffee was an annual event. Green coffee beans joined such other staples as flour and sugar to be picked up in town in 140-pound sacks, loaded onto a horse-drawn wagon and portered back to the farm. There they were stored in a cool "dark room" until the woman of the house was ready to roast them. The beans were spread out in two-inch shallow pans and roasted in a wood-burning oven, with regular shakes administered to ensure consistency of darkness. Many Cajuns remember this ritual of roasting for the rich scents it spread over surrounding fields and marshes.

Roasted almost to black, the beans then were ground by hand and brewed in a French-style drip pot. The thick, strong but mellow coffee was kept on the stove until nightfall and replenished whenever it ran low, ready to provide Cajun men and women with a moment's contemplation and refreshment against the larger backdrop of labor. "Coffee played a big role in our life," remembers Cajun chef Paul Prudhomme. "The first thing you did in the morning was put on water, and the last thing you did at night was take off the pot."

Coffee and the Cuisine of New Orleans

Antoine's opened its doors in 1840, followed over time by other landmarks in the making: Arnaud's, Galatoire's, Begue's, Tujaque's, the list of great restaurants goes on and on. As the nation turned its eyes from the spartan servings on its frontier to the decadent feasts of the French Quarter, simple coffee just wasn't enough anymore—even coffee with ties to the devil, death, love and the ultimate lower depths. The concoctions Creoles produced in their restaurants proved equal to the challenge.

Café noir remained the standard, of course, its boiling water dripped lovingly through linen filters that were washed and hung out to dry. Café au lait also remained popular, even in places so elegant they were more likely to dim the lights for flaming Bananas Foster than to set out a platter of steaming simple beignets. Before long, however, it was *café brûlot* that earned the praise of writers from the civilized but apparently untheatrical north. This heady combination of coffee, brandy and Grand Marnier, cinnamon and cloves, orange and lemon peel made a spectacular finale to a Creole celebration, especially as its ribbon of gold-blue flame followed alcohol down the spiraling orange peel into the bowl of dark brûlot.

• RICH COFFEE, POOR COFFEE

From the very beginning, as farmers and merchants wrestled with a land first seen by explorers, missionaries and fur trappers, Louisiana gained a reputation for drinking its coffee stronger, stranger and usually better than just about anyplace else. Across the southern part of the state, a good cup of coffee has been by definition a strong cup of coffee since the 1700s. When the worldly-wise Ben Franklin imagined the ultimate breakfast, he declared he would go to New Orleans for the perfect cup of coffee. Indeed, there were hotheads in Franklin's time who fought duels over just how their brew should be made— most of them in south Louisiana, where family honor and feminine virtue had a way of coming in second. A full two centuries after Franklin's fantasy, coffee remains an essential element of any memorable New Orleans meal. As proprietress Ella Brennan of Commander's Palace puts it: "You can literally put yourself out of business in New Orleans if you don't serve a good cup of coffee."

With an appreciation of commerce as well as good taste, coffee drinkers realized early that the longer coffee was roasted, the deeper and richer its flavor. They also realized that, since the beans grow lighter as they grow darker, the single argument for the light roast drunk nationwide was that it got more mileage out of each bean, increasing the roaster's profit margin. No Creole or Cajun would stand for this affront to the coin purse as well as the taste buds.

As though this dark roast were not hearty enough, many south Louisiana coffee drinkers have long favored the added taste of chicory—the ground root of the European endive plant.

The Coffee Call, 1863

One of the oldest known plants, chicory was first mentioned in an Egyptian papyrus dating from 4,000 B.C. Aristophanes and Theophrastes consumed great quantities, while Homer longed to refresh himself with "olives and chicory." Suleiman the Magnificent of Turkey is credited as the first to serve this dried ground root with coffee, though he did so only after a palace guard was caught stealing the royal coffee and mixing it with chicory for his own enjoyment.

Gov. James Bowdoin of Massachusetts introduced chicory to the United States in 1785, but his efforts to promote its use in the North paled dramatically beside the popularity of the coffee and chicory of south Louisiana. The legendary Lafcadio Hearn, author of a nineteenth-century cookbook called *La Cuisine Creole*, proclaimed coffee with chicory "the crowning of a grand dinner . . . the pièce de résistance, the greatest pousse-café of all."

Even the slaves of south Louisiana apparently shared a special affection for hot, strong coffee. Many indulgent masters provided beans from time to time, in addition to whole milk and buttermilk. Slaves who earned money were allowed to buy their own coffee, while others less fortunate came up with substitute beverages from cowpeas, sweet potatoes and other ingredients—just as some poor whites did. At first, the Civil War did little to shake this scheme of things, and coffee, like wine, was a fixture at the finest meals. Eventually, however, the Yankee blockade took its toll and even the rich found themselves sipping crushed cowpeas instead of their favorite blend.

By the turn of the century, however, coffee, like the South, was on its way to recovery from the war and Reconstruction, and beans were once again purchased green from the store, roasted to comply with personal taste, then ground up fine for French drip brewing with a grinder turned by hand.

The Fall and Rise of Good Coffee

In many ways, coffee in twentieth-century America has been one long bout between convenience and flavor—with convenience winning virtually every round. While the bean had no doubt suffered abuse in the past at the hands of chuck-wagon cooks on the prairies and hoboes in the teaming railyards, it had seen nothing like the assault on its finer qualities mounted by the coffee manufacturers themselves. Many of today's connoisseurs see the popularization of the pump percolator and instant coffee as distinct downward developments.

Curiously, neither the percolator nor instant coffee had its beginnings in the century that saw its great rise. The first was invented in France by a jeweler named Jacques-Augustin Gandais in 1827. His machine mercifully sprayed the coffee with water just once; it was left to Nicholas Felix Durant to come up with a percolator that raked its boiling water over the grounds time and time again. This method, which came to represent convenience in most American households, produces a brew that is in part "decoction," a throwback to the days when coffee was boiled until it yielded some of its best and most of its worst attributes. The invention of the automatic pump percolator only confirmed for coffee fanatics that the nation's collective genius was on a roll, downward.

With instant, the story was much the same. An early version turned up in some soldiers' saddle bags as early as the Civil War, but it was not until the spread of suburbia and the fascination with everything instant that it took on real roasted coffee in the nation's consumption statistics. Some coffee experts insist that the very process used to make the granules is objectionable, since it involves extracting a concentrated brew from ground coffee, then removing the liquid using some form of dehydration. The residue, which is heralded as instant, is 100 percent coffee to be sure but coffee that includes much more of the grounds' properties than is considered acceptable in terms of taste. The simple reason for such efficiency: higher profits. Each bean is literally drained of more coffee flavor —50 percent of its soluble solids rather than 19 percent in ground coffees—and the result is more bitterness as well. Despite continued improvement of the technology involved, from the primitive dehydration of seventy years ago to today's freeze-drying, the product continues to be an affront to many of coffee's staunchest supporters.

While it had been in the works for years, the gourmet coffee revolution got an unintended and slightly perverse push in 1975 by a series of severe shocks to the coffee drinker's pocketbook. The world's coffee stockpile had been depleted over a decade when a sudden killer frost struck the prime growing regions of Brazil, destroying millions of coffee trees and up to 70 percent of the year's crop. A month after the Brazilian frost, a three-sided civil war broke out in Angola, cutting the harvest there by about 30 percent. Floods in Colombia knocked off up to 20 percent of its coffee crop, while an earthquake in Guatemala delivered a serious blow to its supply. Finally, a deadly plant disease called coffee rust had a go at whatever sections of Central America had sidestepped earlier disasters.

Not surprisingly, coffee prices rose sharply in the

United States and elsewhere, forcing even the hardiest drinkers to rethink their beverage habits. For a time, teas and colas found new life in the marketplace—and both had enjoyed great popularity even before the roof came crashing in on coffee. At the same time, however, the gourmet coffee movement took root, one that recognized the high price of pleasure and decided to pay it after all. This willingness, coupled with an expanding appreciation of fine wines and the growth of the gourmet food market in general, helped coffee take on a whole new meaning to thousands of Americans. As high prices and a new series of caffeine scares wrestled down overall consumption, the sales of gourmet coffees marketed by origin and savored for their individuality asserted a dramatic rise in the 1980s.

From Tree to Table

The Beans

The object of these centuries of controversy is actually a small, unassuming fruit that rather resembles a cherry. On the outside is a skin called the pulp, followed by a sweet-tasting gummy substance surrounding each of two flat-sided beans—or occasionally a single rounded one. Each of these beans is wrapped in a tough outer "parchment" and a delicate inner "silver skin." Usually, all four of these natural protective coverings are removed before the "brown gold" leaves the plantation.

The tree itself, which scientists have named *Coffea' arabica*, is native only to Ethiopia and Kenya. Yet, having been transplanted, it also grows well in Java, Sumatra and other islands of the old Netherlands Indies; in India and Africa; Latin America and the West Indies. There are as many as eight species of coffee sharing general characteristics, but only three turn up in the coffee lover's search for the perfect brew—and only two regularly.

Arabica. The bean most important to coffee commerce, the one from which the finest unblended coffee is made,

Coffee plant from Strässle's Naturgeschichte, *1885*

shares its name with the trees on which all types are grown, *Coffea arabica*. It is found most often in tropical regions, though it can be grown in temperate climates as well. Requiring shade in hot, low-lying districts, it can do without shade nicely at its preferred higher altitudes. Yet the fruit of a single tree yields only 1½ or 2 pounds of coffee a year.

Robusta. Discovered originally in the Belgian Congo (now Zaire), the bean known as *Coffea robusta* has become increasingly significant to the trade, even though its flavor offers little or no comparison to that of *arabica*. The reasons for its success are hardiness and fertility. *Robusta* trees can be grown successfully at lower altitudes than *arabica*. Each *robusta* tree produces enough fruit for 4 pounds of coffee within two or three years of planting. The commercial prospects are so tempting that many growers have replaced *arabica* lost to frost or disease with *robusta*.

Liberica. The third species of bean that turns up in current coffee literature bears the appropriate name *liberica* since it finds few boosters outside the African nation of Liberia where it is grown. The bean belongs to the *robusta* school of sturdiness but produces a crop even smaller than the respected *arabica.* With consumers spurning its poor taste and farmers rejecting its poor yield, the future of *Coffea liberica* is anything but bright.

Best Conditions

Coffee thrives where the mean annual temperature is seventy degrees Fahrenheit; readings below fifty-five and higher than eighty tend to cause problems. The plant can grow from sea level all the way up to 7,000 feet (the frost line in the tropics), with *arabica* claiming the cooler highlands and leaving the hotter, wetter slopes to its popular but poorer relation, *robusta.*

The experts stress that coffee needs sunshine but never more than a few hours each day, making hilly country the best place for it to grow. This alternation of sunlight and shadow can also be found in areas where cloud cover and mist drift through the mountains, protecting plants from prolonged encounters with the burning sun. When all else fails, shade trees are planted in groves of coffee trees.

All coffees favor the same chemical composition of soil; it is the means nature and man use to achieve this composition that vary so dramatically. Since the soil should be rich in potash, nitrogen and phosphoric acid, soil made up of decomposed mold, organic matter and disintegrated volcanic rock is best. The lava part is easy on Hawaii, for example, but the additional nutrients must be brought in from other points on the big island. The Brazilians grow coffee in their famous *terra roxa,* which gets its name from the red topsoil that covers a layer peppered with gravel. The rolling terrain of Java varies from loamy topsoil over a porous subsoil to rich dirt strewn with layers of rock. Either setting has proven rich in nutrients, and each shows a special talent for mixing moisture and drainage in the most favorable of proportions.

A delicate balance is required, indeed. Too much water is disastrous, as it encourages the wood of the coffee plant to develop instead of its flowers and fruits. Too little water and nothing develops, a condition that usually proves fatal. A constant misty rain is the ideal, since it keeps only a sheen of moisture on the plants and in the soil. Farmers like rainfall of seventy inches a year, distributed as evenly through the year as possible.

Even when soil and moisture are nothing short of perfect, coffee farmers can find themselves at the mercy of frost, insects or disease. Frosts like the one that devastated Brazil in 1975 and sent world coffee prices into the stratosphere freeze the sap in the trees; the leaves, branches and roots rupture as the sap expands. The trees die when the cold snap ends and the sap streams out through these ruptures.

The dreaded *broca*, or coffee-bean borer, is the single worst insect enemy, though it has found a destructive ally in the coffee-leaf miner, which feeds on tender new leaves rather than the bean itself. Among the diseases giving farmers fits, one called *Hemileia vastatrix* is the most vicious. This is the unstoppable illness that wiped out Ceylon's thriving coffee industry in the 1870s. Pessimists keep predicting that *Hemileia* will turn up in the Western Hemisphere, but so far it has not.

Hands That Touch Coffee

Coffee is picked when the cherry turns crimson, eight or nine months after blossoming. Then, the beans must be picked quickly because when overripe they shrink and dry out and are then unusable. On most large plantations entire families, including young children, join in the picking, moving deftly between the rows and tossing mature beans into baskets slung over their shoulders. The baskets are emptied at stations or into wagons that hurry along behind the field laborers. The world's best coffee pickers can manage a day's harvest of 200 to 250 pounds. The practice of hand picking is nearly universal; the technological innovations that have changed other industries

so dramatically are unknown to the coffee business. All cherries do not ripen at once, forcing the pickers to return five or six times to clean a tree. Since the harvest almost invariably occurs during the rainy season, this labor is not only backbreaking but uncomfortably wet as well. It all adds up to a job that is easily abandoned when others are available—such as those created by the tourism booms of Hawaii and Puerto Rico. Labor is now scarce on coffee plantations in such countries. In remote and depressed economies, plantation owners are able to exploit the fact that theirs is the only game around.

Two Means to One End

History and ingenuity have given the world a pair of distinctly different methods for achieving a single desired result. Both methods—one ancient, the other relatively modern—involve fermentation of the coffee cherry, followed by the removal of the outer covering in a way that will eventually please buyers, shippers, roasters, and drinkers around the world.

Dry method. Used by the Arabs in Yemen, the dry method is the oldest known route from picked to prepared bean. The ancient Arabs allowed the sun to shrivel the fruit on the tree, then shook the beans onto cloths spread out on the ground. Today, a full 65 percent of the world's coffee is still prepared in a way that resembles the ancient methods.

In Yemen and Ethiopia, beans still dry on the tree, but other countries using the dry method give picked beans an initial washing and spread them in thin layers over drying grounds for two to three weeks. Fermentation takes place, while the beans are turned by rakes several times a day to ensure uniformity of exposure and are covered at night for protection from moisture. When the beans are completely dry, they are sent to milling machines for removal of husk, parchment and silver skin. The green bean emerges, ready for the marketplace. Most Brazilian coffees are processed by the dry method, as of course are Mocha from Yemen and Djimmah from Ethiopia.

Wet method. Not surprisingly, the more modern wet method was pioneered in countries with abundant water and some industrialization; while its goals are much the same as the dry method's, its processes are much more strictly controlled. The wet method results in more finely flavored (and higher priced) coffees, including Colombian, Costa Rican, Guatemalan, Venezuelan, Mexican, Kenyan, Tanzanian, Kona from Hawaii and Kivi from Zaire.

Coffee beans prepared by this more costly method are washed, then put into machines that strip away the exterior fruit pulp and expose the sticky substance inside. The berries are left to ferment in large, spotless concrete tanks, an accelerated process that takes from twelve to twenty-four hours, then washed with constantly changing water in concrete sluiceways or special washing machines. After drying, either naturally in the sun or with a machine that applies a current of hot air, they are transferred to hulling machines, where the parchment and silver skin are removed.

The potential dangers of the wet method are improper drying, which produces a rancid taste, and overfermentation caused either by belated removal from the concrete tanks or incomplete washing following removal. Yet the entire process is a far more premeditated way of doing business, and far more likely to produce consistently pleasant results than the dry method.

How Big? How Pure?

Wet method or dry, the process used to prepare the beans is crucial to their final quality. Yet there remain two steps—sizing and hand sorting—that decide to a large extent what price these prepared beans bring on the world market.

In modern commercial practice, grading according to size is done by machines that transport the beans across a series of sieves of different sized holes. The beans simply drop through the holes of the corresponding size, separating themselves into five or more grades. These grades almost always include triage, third flats, second flats, first flats and first and second peaberries, though "elephant" and "mother" sizes are sometimes picked out as well. All over the coffee-growing world, the philosophy and necessity of this step is the same, even if the vocabulary differs wildly. Grades are significant. The larger ones pull a higher price because they are more consistent, prettier and rarer. Large beans make it easier to spot and remove defective ones.

After separation on the basis of size, the beans still must be picked over by hand to remove those that are faulty or discolored. In many countries, the beans are spread out on a belt that speeds past a line of women and children. In others, the preference is for a small machine that lets a single person handle the job, running his moving belt with a treadle. The very finest coffee is very fine in part because it is usually picked over twice, making the beans that end up at market all the more elite in character.

Taste Tells It All

What follows for each coffee bean is a dizzying odyssey through international commerce—transporting, warehousing, buying and selling, financing, mixing and bagging, weighing and marking, shipping, importing and distributing. At each important step of the journey, there are men who accept or reject based on taste. Called simply "tasters," these fellows apply a rather bizarre ritual to deciding which coffee makes it to groceries and gourmet shops for your consideration.

They sit hunched over a large round table with a revolving lazy Susan top. They roast the beans in batches, grind them and measure out ground coffee into an immaculate cup and douse it with boiling water. They inhale the full fragrance of the brew, then with a violent sucking noise spray a spoonful across the back of their tongues. After testing a coffee for body, smoothness, mellowness or acidity, they spit the entire amount into a high brass receptacle called a gaboon, strategically positioned nearby.

Despite a growing preference for brews from a single type of bean, the fact remains that nearly all the coffees sold are blends of various origins and grades. Tasters play an essential role in maintaining a blend's balance of taste and texture—not to mention its balance of trade. With the wide variety of beans available, flavor and cost become the overriding concerns, caught on an eternally sliding scale of compromise. Even when a new blend is judged superb, the taster's job is anything but complete. He must continually assess the component parts, assuring that the quality of each remains as consistent as possible, and find substitutes if the taste goes down or the price goes up.

An English street coffee stall

A User's Guide
to Fine Coffee

Finding the Right Roast

There was a time, of course, when just about everyone roasted coffee beans at home. There was little choice in the matter, since the beans were sold green. Yet even with the element of personality an individual might bring to the roasting, it is generally believed that handling this chore at home was always more a matter of necessity than preference. Some modern connoisseurs insist on roasting their own, assuring both freshness and the precise level of darkness they desire. But in fact, unlike home grinding, home roasting is more trouble than it's worth.

For starters, proper coffee roasting is nothing less than an art, one requiring expertise and no small amount of love. There is a magic moment when the bean stands revealed in all its flavor and aroma. Miss that moment, ignore the signs that only experience can distinguish, and the batch is well on its way to disaster. While knowing the roast you like best is important, that knowledge does not translate directly into an ability to achieve it in the roasting pan. Most specialty shops encourage their customers to taste their way through the various roasts, making decisions based on their individual preferences but leaving the precarious job of roasting to the people and equipment best suited for it.

Any shop that roasts coffee is free within the boundaries of commerce to call it virtually anything. No single international organization lays down a law of coffee names, yet there are some standard descriptions of roasting, and a current movement that favors further standardization based on numerical gradations rather than ethnic origins of beans. The following descriptions are based on a nomenclature that travels at least part of the distance toward a numerical spectrum, creating roasts from light medium to espresso. Ultimately the quest for a favorite roast will depend on taste buds to draw conclusions beyond the power of words.

Light medium. Also called American, brown or city roast, this is the basic darkness used in most national brands. Largely because of its market saturation, it is the roast that most Americans assume they prefer. Yet it often lacks the brilliance of darker roasts, so the curious are encouraged to forge ahead.

Medium. This is a Community Kitchens specialty roast that does not coincide precisely with any roast available on a national basis. It is slightly darker in appearance than American roast, and slightly darker in taste as well.

Medium dark. Nationwide, there is a great deal of variation in this roast, which is also sometimes known as Vienna. It is halfway between the medium and the dark roast favored in France, while still a long way from the darkest roasts loved in Italy. A mix of half medium- and half dark-roasted beans similarly produces a rich-tasting brew without the body of its brethren farther down the scale.

Dark. This is often called French roast, or even New Orleans roast, since it is to this coffee that Creoles add their chicory. The color of semisweet chocolate, it comes close to espresso in flavor without sacrificing smoothness. It exhibits peak flavor in the cup, along with a full measure of body.

Espresso. This, the darkest of all roasts, is known nationally as Italian. Beans roasted in this manner are black (though not scorched), with a surface that is shiny and oily. This coffee offers the deepest flavor of all.

People embarking on an experiment in coffee roasts are reminded that darker does not mean stronger. Though the darker roasts usually exhibit more pronounced tastes, the strength of coffee is determined solely by the amount of soluble solids extracted from the grounds. At first, this distinction may seem like mere semantics; but as the palate becomes better educated, questions relating to strength should not be allowed to confuse comparisons of fullness or acidity.

Secondly, anyone interested in determining preference honestly should be aware that the cards of commerce are stacked in favor of light roasts. It's a simple fact that the longer a bean is roasted, the more it swells and loses weight with result of more beans to the pound. It is more profitable, therefore, to sell heavier, light roasted coffee since more of each purchased bean makes it into the stores. The overriding concern of the coffee lover, however, is taste, not cost. The perfect roast may be waiting in the darker variations preferred almost universally outside the United States,

Beyond the Same Old Grind

If roasting is better done by those who really know how, the grinding of coffee matches its sentimental allure with a solid consumer advantage. Whole coffee beans will simply stay fresh longer than ground coffee stored under similar conditions, delivering the finest in flavor when brewed. Freshly roasted beans are at their best when they are freshly ground. Ultimately, the greatest value—based on pleasure returned on investment— may be the ideal roast combined with home grinding.

Coffee beans can be kept in home freezers for several months, as long as they are dry and sealed away from other flavors. Freezing is especially useful for people who purchase several pounds at a time by mail or who live too

Bicycle coffee mill, English cartoon, 1869

far from their supplier to stock up often. Coffee beans stored in this manner, and indeed ground coffee that is stored as well, need not be thawed before grinding and brewing. Ground coffee bought in a vacuum pack will usually stay fresh for months, but once the seal is broken, speedy consumption or special care is called for. Opened packages should be stored in airtight containers and will be fine in the refrigerator if less than a pound a week is used.

As is not true with roasting, the degrees of grinding are related more to chemistry and physics than to personal taste. There is little other reason, for example, to prefer a fine grind to a drip or regular grind than what best suits the coffee maker you prefer. The grind controls the length of time it takes to achieve the optimum 19 percent extraction. A grind that allows that to happen in the time it takes a coffee maker to complete its brewing cycle is, quite simply, the proper grind. Don't devote a lot of time to meditating on this, however. Follow the directions on your coffee maker or ask your specialty coffee dealer for guidance.

Here are the three most common commercial coffee grinds, along with descriptions of their recommended use.

Fine. This grind, with a brewing cycle of just one to four minutes, is used almost exclusively in espresso and in so-called Greek or Turkish coffee—in which the grounds are drunk along with the extracted liquid.

Drip. Halfway between fine and regular, this grind takes its name from the type of coffee pot to which its four- to six-minute brewing time is best suited. It turns up most spectacularly in the beloved coffees of France and south Louisiana.

Regular. The coarsest of the three most commonly available grinds, this one also has the longest brewing cycle—from six to eight minutes. As such, it is best suited for the modern pump percolator.

While all three of these grinds include particles of various sizes, those with the highest percentage of small pieces are known as fine and those with the lowest are called regular, with drip falling midway between the two. Basically, determine the brewing cycle of your particular coffee maker and choose the grind to match.

The Perfect Cup

It is still possible, even with fine coffee freshly roasted and ground, to turn out something no more memorable than a warm, brown drink if something goes wrong in the brewing. According to the now defunct Coffee Brewing Institute, the only real secrets lie in knowing the exact proportion of coffee and water, as well as the length of time contact between the two should be maintained. People who grind their own coffee or buy on the basis of proper grind are halfway home already. The rest is a question of consistency.

As for the proportion, best results are nearly always achieved by using two level measuring teaspoons of coffee to three-quarters measuring cup or six fluid ounces of water. The institute developed the Approved Coffee Measure (ACM in the trade) to go with each six ounces of water.

Every brew should begin with a thoroughly clean coffee pot rinsed with hot water just before preparation. Other

Egyptian coffee service (above) and charcoal heater (below)

wise, the coffee oils that form a nearly invisible film on the inside walls of the coffee maker will sabotage each new batch with rancid flavor. Coffee makers should be disassembled for washing and cleaned with a mild detergent or baking soda and water, then rinsed out completely.

If freshly ground coffee is essential, so is freshly drawn cold water. Water, after all, accounts for 98.75 percent of the average cup. It must be cold because heating and standing in tanks and pipes make it flat. While naturally soft water wins highest honors, artificially softened water is to be avoided with a vengeance because chemical additives also flatten the taste. Any water treatment that unduly increases the contact time between liquid and coffee should be shunned, as of course should any water with undesirable tastes or odors.

The temperature of the water should be just above 200 degrees Fahrenheit when it hits the coffee, but this is far less a perfectionist fetish than it might at first seem. Actually, this only takes quick action, since water retreats from boiling to this temperature as soon as it is removed from the heat. He who hesitates risks losing the proper extraction and balance. Coffee itself should never be allowed to boil. An unpleasant change in flavor occurs when it does.

Finally, all coffee should be served as soon as it is brewed. Oxidation over time takes a heavy toll in aroma, and the taste becomes flat and eventually bitter. If a temperature of 185 to 190 degrees is maintained, coffee may be held up to an hour without serious damage. But never, say the experts, reheat coffee that has gotten cold; the violent temperature shifts are more than good coffee can survive.

Teaching the Tastebuds

A good coffee deserves all the attention you would give a good wine. While both beverages begin as fruit on a tree, the similarities begin in earnest with the fermentation needed for processing. Fermentation, which separates and elevates wine above any other fate to which a grape could aspire, plays a major role in coffee's life as well—especially in the wet or washed processing that removes the fruit from the seed. This fermentation imparts an acidity to the taste that can be contrasted from coffee to coffee. In recent years, connoisseurs have started referring to this acidity as a particular brew's "wineyness"— first, because it sidesteps acidity's negative connotation, and second because it stresses the fellowship with wine and connoisseurship in general.

Beyond these similarities, there is another that becomes increasingly significant with the expansion of each coffee drinker's knowledge and sensitivity to taste. Like grapes, coffee draws its most important characteristics from the terrain in which it grows. The quality of the soil, the moisture in the air, the amount and intensity of sunlight help fashion the complex interplay that eventually strikes each drinker's palate. Each setting signs its name to the coffee it produces, a signature identical to no other in the world. For the coffee lover, as for the lover of wines, the search for the perfect taste is an adventure in armchair travel, a game of compare and contrast that turns disappointing from time to time but in the end leaves only delight.

Timing and fate play a role as well, as they do in making great years for some wines and disastrous years for others. Weather has a tremendous impact on coffee, so dramatic changes are reflected in the cup even without human intervention. In 1983–1984, for example, terrible rains spawned by the El Niño current in the Pacific Ocean cut drastically into the number of fine beans available from Brazil, making them considerably harder to find and much more expensive for drinkers who did. Beyond the size of a crop, however, weather conditions can affect the taste of coffee from season to season. Coffee taste often can be kept consistent through a masterful juggling of the blend, though a single-bean coffee drunk year after year will change considerably over time, even within a single crop. So it is completely reasonable to expect that as understanding of gourmet coffee grows, so will conversation about this year's fantastic Harar or that year's disappointing Sumatran.

In seeking your favorite coffee bean—indeed in loving each day of the search—you should establish an awareness of how fine coffees are judged. This is more than a clever cocktail party vocabulary; it is a set of concepts that positions world coffees in relation to each other so that important comparisons can be made. As with most other coffee concepts, the nomenclature changes from country to country, even from taster to taster within a single firm. But it is easy to follow the reasoning and establish guidelines of your own.

There are, by most accounts, four basic attributes ascribed to coffee, a quartet of qualities that rise or fall independent of each other. Among connoisseurs, each coffee is judged on these even as it is enjoyed, providing a basis for instant comparison and also for pragmatic memory. A coffee that pleases in one or more areas is a good bet to try again, and it points the way to others in its immediate family. A coffee that disappoints or seriously displeases is one to avoid in the future—often, for better or worse, along with its relatives. The four attributes are aroma, acidity (wineyness), body and flavor.

Aroma. This, of course, is a natural spinoff of other coffee qualities. Yet like a wine's distinctive bouquet, it takes on a life of its own. In fact, coffee aroma goes wine one better, since it fills the room during brewing in a way no amount of breathing of wine could ever produce. For the most part, coffees smell the way they taste. But a few coffees—Colombian most notably—are more fragrant than the rest.

Acidity. Though this book groups coffees by their wineyness, it's best to address the concept here as the chemistry it really is. Coffee lovers never mean sour when they refer to a brew as "acidy." What they are communicating is a tartness, a snap that titillates the palate in ways reminiscent of white wine. Even in the ranks of acidy coffees, there are undeniable (and enjoyable) differences. No one, for example, would taste a Mexican coffee, a Sumatran, an Ethiopian and a Tanzanian and proclaim their twist identical.

Body. Compare olive oil to vinegar, or maple syrup to vodka, and you have a sense of body. This is the feeling of heaviness or thickness that gives each coffee a unique identity on the palate. It works with coffee as it does with wine. Whatever their other attributes, Burgundies are heavier in body than clarets, red wines heavier than white. Sumatran coffees generally are heaviest, with Mexican or Venezuelan at the other end of the scale. In general, people who add milk to their coffee should seek out the heavier brews so the flavor and feeling will survive.

Flavor. Though this attribute tends to be ambiguous, related as it is to all the others, it remains for most coffee drinkers the most important. When the beverage is consumed—sipped or sucked, by neophyte or professional—the question of flavor is paramount. Do you *like* this coffee? In this area, each person puts together his own vocabulary, with words like "mild" or "mellow" contrasted with words like "harsh" or "hard." Mother Nature gets a nod in descriptions like "grassy" or "earthy," as does the critic in each of us whenever "most distinctive" or "least distinctive" is used.

Of course, the freshness of the coffee beans affects all these attributes. Unfortunately, there is no easy way for the consumer to be sure the coffee beans he buys are as fresh as possible. Most gourmet coffee is roasted by a number of small-scale roasters throughout the country and distributed regionally. A few, but not many, deal directly with growers in various countries, but most buy through brokers. At the point of purchase, the consumer should look for beans that are kept in covered bins rather than open burlap bags, which expose the coffee to the air. The roasting and distribution of coffee is constant, rather than seasonal, so it might help to ask your supplier when he received his last shipment. Obviously, a high-volume shop is likeliest to have the freshest supply. The rather newly developed valve bags, which allow air to escape but do not let in oxygen or moisture—which destroy flavor—are excellent for preserving freshness, but they are not available at most sources of fine coffee beans.

Coffee pot, Vienna, 1840

A Bean Baedeker

Gourmet coffees fall into three distinctive types:

WINEY, HEAVY BODY

This group takes in quite a few of the best coffees from antiquity, including Ethiopian Harar and Yemen Mocha.

Yet there are strong signs that these brews are losing ground to both the milder and drier coffees as consumers seek greater smoothness. This factor is especially important for drinkers who fill huge mugs to the brim, and fill them again and again, rather than sip at a demitasse of devil's brew. For people more familiar with wine than coffee, winey brews compare to young white wines and contrast with smooth-tasting older reds. Winey coffees are by their nature acidic, so people who drink great quantities in short order or have difficulty with acids in general might do well to steer clear.

Colombian

In the words of one coffee lover, Colombian is for people who long for a Rolls but can afford only a BMW. Colombia's "mild" coffees have catapulted it into second place behind Brazil in total world production. With 12 percent of the U.S. market, Colombia still is a fair distance behind Brazil, which claims 30 to 35 percent, but its combination of high mountain cultivation, careful hand picking and modern wet processing has earned it high marks from connoisseurs. At its best, Colombian rivals Guatemalan and Costa Rican. Its wineyness stops far short of Ethiopian; the tones call up memories of Africa's finest, though they never overwhelm.

Three mountain ranges or *cordilleras* trisect central Colombia from north to south, creating its coffee-growing regions. The beans grown in the central and eastern sections are the best of the Colombian crop. The central *cordillera*'s most respected coffees, named for the towns through which they are marketed, are Medellín, Armenia and Manizales. Medellín is most famous of this trio, with its heavy body, rich flavor and balanced wineyness. Moving to the eastern *cordillera*, the finest coffees are Bogotá (named for the region surrounding the Colombian capital, nearly as flavorful as Medellín) and Bucaramanga, a soft-bean coffee similar to the finest Sumatran for body, acidity and flavor. Grading of Colombian coffee starts with *supremo* and works down; yet for the convenience of commercial buyers, an additional comprehensive grade called *excelso* has been created from *supremo* and runner-up *extra,* along with peaberries and caracol (a peaberry selection) of both grades.

Ethiopian Harar

Drinking Ethiopian coffee is a true celebration of "roots," since the whole love affair began with a few trees growing wild sometime before the ninth century. The town of Kaffa gets a linguistic tip of the hat each time coffee is ordered anywhere. Today, Ethiopia produces a healthy crop of more than two million bags each year, yet domestic consumption is so high that less than half of that finds its way into the export market. Coffee provides more than 60 percent of the nation's export income, even with more mountains of coffee beans going unpicked for lack of access roads. Ethiopian production could be tripled without planting a single new tree.

Harar is sometimes described as coffee for people who favor excitement over subtlety, as well as for those with numb palates. It is, by all accounts, the winiest coffee in the world—possessing a strong, gamey flavor reminiscent of a dry country wine. Harar easily brushes aside the winiest Colombian and even the most persistent Mocha, yet its body and greater acidity make it lack Mocha's balance. Usually sold in the United States as simply "Ethiopian," this coffee is grown at 5,000 to 6,000 feet on plantations near the old capital of Harar, or Harari. It also turns up variously as "Ethiopian Harar," "Longberry Harar," "Shortberry Harar," even "Mocha Harar"—though this last should never be confused with the real Mocha from Yemen. The Longberry is the most highly regarded. Since Harar accounts for no more than 13 percent of Ethiopia's crop (with the rest being milder, wild-grown varieties), there is a great deal of uncertainty over how much actually makes it to any foreign shore. The world's oldest nation of coffee drinkers shares little of its finest with the United States, though the best chance of finding Harar seems to exist on the West Coast. Those who stumble on a batch should try to confirm it is "new crop" Ethiopian, since the very pungency that makes it interesting fades quickly with age. The serving of "past crop" Ethiopian is a dull occasion indeed.

Ethiopian Wild

Coming from the country that produces Harar on plantations at 5,000 to 6,000 feet, the wild coffees of Ethiopia seem doomed to be ugly ducklings, or at least perennial bridesmaids. The beans tend to be scrawny, making an unattractive roast. They also tend to be carelessly picked and poorly processed by the dry method used in Ethiopia since the dawn of coffee's history. Yet some coffee lovers look beyond their bland taste (relative to the super-winey Harar) and find in them a touch of excitement, even of exoticism. As the name implies, coffees classed as Ethiopian Wild are not cultivated at all, merely gathered from the mountainsides. All are of the *arabica* variety, with the most interesting beans growing at altitudes of 4,000 to 6,000 feet around the towns of Agaro, Gore, Gimbi and Lekemti in the district of Djimmah. Coffee also grows wild and is harvested by natives in the Sidamo district.

Chances are slim for running across these wild-grown coffees in any American specialty store. Those beans that do turn up are labeled Ethiopian (as opposed to Ethiopian Harar) or perhaps Abyssinian. Though often dismissed as a novelty, the Wilds do share with their more celebrated, cultivated relatives a winey pungency that harks back to coffee's beginnings. The best advice is to taste a cup unblended first, then consider it for a blend with richer, heavier coffees like Colombian or Java. Ethiopian Wild is excellent for blends that include dark-roasted coffee.

Guatemalan Antigua, Cobán

Some of the world's most distinctively flavored coffees hail from the central highlands of Guatemala. A full half of the nation's two million bags a year are grown on tiny farms putting out fewer than forty bags a year. All Guatemalan coffees are washed *arabica*, and all, like Costa Rican, are classed according to the altitude at which they are grown. There is almost never a mention of growing district—simply a numerical reference between 1,000 and 5,500 feet. The best coffees grown in Guatemala are almost exclusively exported to Europe, so the opportunity to taste some anywhere should be seized.

The two names to conjure with here are Antigua, from

the dramatic countryside around the old Guatemalan capital, and Cobán, from the Alta Verapaz district a hundred miles to the northeast. Both exhibit a spicy flavor that strikes almost all drinkers as intriguing. The finest Guatemalan coffees are medium to full in richness and very rich in flavor. When buying coffee from these highlands, it's a simple case of the higher the better. "Strictly hard bean," grown at 4,500 feet or higher, is the finest grade, followed by "hard bean" at 4,000 to 4,500 feet. Antigua and Cobán come from the districts growing the winiest, most heavily flavored coffees in the country.

Kenya

Kenya is only a few hundred miles south of Ethiopia and Yemen, where coffee first distinguished itself, but the art of cultivation arrived much later via the Germans and then the British. Though much Kenyan coffee is still raised on tiny plots, the modern industry that prepares it for sale rivals and perhaps surpasses such giants as Colombia. Kenya produces about a million bags of its mild coffee —entirely of the *arabica* variety—every year, with only about 10 percent of that exported finding its way to the United States. The nation's output has always been popular in Europe, particularly among its former British and West German growers, as well as in Sweden and the Netherlands. Together, these countries have been known to cart off more than half the Kenyan crop.

Like the Harar from Ethiopia and the Mocha from Yemen, Kenyan exhibits a winey, dry aftertaste that can be quite distinctive. At its best, it surpasses Harar and even Mocha in full-bodied richness. It is considered a fine coffee for seekers of the striking, the unusual. All coffees exported from Kenya are graded by quality in the cup by the Liquoring Department of the Kenya Coffee Board, starting with AA and working down to A and B. Most Kenyan coffee appearing in specialty coffee shops comes from the central region around 17,000-foot Mount Kenya, though some is qualified with the name of the country's capital city, Nairobi. There is also a small growing region along the border with Uganda, but the coffee from those slopes tends to be at once inferior and impossible to find.

First-time adventurers would do well to stick with Kenyan AA.

Tanzanian

Tanzanian coffee shares a large part of its history with Kenyan, since its industry harks back to the same early developers from Germany and England. Today, 40 percent of the country's 600,000 to 800,000 bags a year are exported to the United States, though only about two-thirds of the crop is *arabica*. The *robusta* comes principally from districts called Bukoba and Karagive, so these names should be avoided if they turn up at all. The best Tanzanians grow on the slopes of Mount Kilimanjaro in Moshi, as well as on mounts Meru and Oldeani. Smaller amounts of *arabica* are grown much farther south, between Lake Tanganyika and Lake Malawi. Coffees from the main region may be named after the mountain on which they are grown, or they may be called Moshi or Arusha after their nearest main towns and shipping points. The southern growths are usually designated Mbeya, after one of that region's principal towns.

Among coffee lovers, Tanzanian has something to please two distinct tastes. Most of its coffees tend to have the sharpness, the acidity associated with Africa and Arabia. They are medium- to full-bodied and fairly rich in flavor. Others, however, seem related to coffees from Sumatra and Celebes—comfortably rich, full-bodied but lacking much of the winey quality their geography would lead you to expect. As with Kenyan, AA is the highest grade from Tanzania, followed by A and B.

Yemen Mocha

Appreciating true Mocha requires a talent for slicing through confusion. The name today can be applied to all the earth's coffees in antiquated slang, to all coffees grown in Yemen and indeed the rest of Arabia, and even to a drink made of equal parts of coffee and hot chocolate. The fault in this lies in history, in the long and colorful tale of coffee cultivation in this ancient part of the world. Despite centuries of misunderstanding, however, and transplanting to regions thousands of miles removed,

Mocha is still grown much as it was in 600 A.D., cultivated on irrigated terraces carved into semi-arid mountainsides and dried with the fruit still attached to the beans. The dried husk is removed later by millstone or some other primitive machinery, giving the bean a rough, irregular look. The tiny Mocha crop, which took its name from an inconsequential port on the Red Sea, finds its way out today through the ports of Aden and Hodeida. Annual export to the United States is small enough to be considered 0 percent of the coffee bought by Americans, yet the gourmet coffee movement is finally giving it its due.

Like the name Mocha itself, delineations of coffee grown in Yemen defy all attempts at agreement. No one seems to agree on how to designate grade, district or variety of bean, so it's best to rely on a simple ranking that seems to please even the most discerning palate. Mattari is the best Yemen Mocha, with Sharki running a close second and Sanani a comfortable third. The plantation coffees of Yemen join those of Ethiopia and some from Kenya and Tanzania as the winiest in the world. Yet if Mexican coffees elicit comparison to dry, white wines, Mochas and Ethiopians remind many of Bordeaux—with an unmistakable aftertaste left on the palate as a souvenir of acidity. In addition, for all the bristling among coffee lovers over such a populist comparison, Mochas do indeed exhibit a strange additional flavor associated with chocolate. If it's this rich edge to the aftertaste that pleases most with Mocha, a stronger-than-usual brew would be in order. Complex and character-rich in the cup, this coffee surpasses even Ethiopian for heavy body yet balances this with a smoothness its nearest cousin lacks.

DRY, HEAVY BODY

There are only a handful of distinguished coffees in this category, but they are interesting for at least two reasons. They demand attention for uniqueness alone, offering a taste and texture quite different from the winey, full-bodied coffees and the milder, light-bodied ones. And they introduce into the gourmet coffee market two examples from the busiest coffee-producing country in the world, Brazil, which otherwise is noted for quantity rather than quality. These beans produce a brew at the other end of the spectrum from the winey, full-bodied coffees that displease some drinkers with their heavily fermented, even grassy taste. They can be smooth in the manner of mild coffees yet provide the body necessary for some drinkers' full satisfaction. All this results from the dry or unwashed method of processing, which sidesteps much of the fermented taste produced by the wet method. Some fermentation occurs as the beans dry out in the sun, lending a special, but not intrusive flavor.

Brazilian Bourbon Santos; Small Bean Peaberry

Brazil is unquestionably the coffee capital of the world. It produces more coffee than any other country—and it is capable of producing even more. It also turns out such a numbing variety of beans that referring to them as "Brazilians" is, some insist, even worse than meaningless, since it implies some family of characteristics that does not begin to exist. A full third of Brazil is suitable for coffee growing, in a region that extends from the Amazon in the north to the southern borders of the states of Paraná and São Paulo, and from the Atlantic coast to the western boundary of the state of Mato Grosso. Coffee is cultivated in seventeen of the country's twenty-one states, but the fact of the matter is that four states alone produce 98 percent of the crop. Nearly half the coffee grown in all Brazil hails from Paraná, with São Paulo making a major contribution and Minas Gerais joining Espírito Santo to fill in around the edges. Other states that might turn up in discussions of Brazilian coffee include Rio de Janeiro, Mato Grosso, Pernambuco, Bahia, Goías and Ceará. Most Brazilian coffees are *arabica*, and nearly all are processed by the ancient dry method. The beans are grown on 300,000 farms, most on plateaus ranging in altitude from 1,800 to 4,000 feet. Two factors have joined forces in recent years to undercut even greater domination of the world market—a string of weather disasters culminating in the great frost of 1975, and a diversification program that led to the destruction of billions of trees. Though supplying up to 35 percent of the world's coffee is an impressive bit of commerce, that figure is down from more than 60 percent earlier in the century.

The finest Brazilian coffees are hard to find and often overlooked because of the small part they play in the country's huge production. Drinkers who know better are outraged by claims that a blend is "100 percent Brazilian," since this implies a selectivity contrary to fact. As such, most of its coffees are palatable and perhaps a little better. In this century, Minas coffee from the southern region of Minas Gerais and Santos grown in the region of Araraquarense in the state of São Paulo have emerged to attract attention from the gourmet trade. Named for one of its principal shipping ports, the bean comes mainly from the original Bourbon strain of *Coffea arabica* brought in the eighteenth century from what is now the island of Réunion. The small, curly bean is the highest grade Brazil produces, and it is likely to be the only Brazilian offered by a specialty shop. Bourbon Santos is smooth in flavor, medium in body and moderate in wineyness.

Small Bean Peaberry is a variation on Santos, a rounded bean from an occasional coffee cherry rather than the usual flat-sided pair. The peaberry taste is a property unto itself, a special sweetness and clarity that can be quite interesting. Yet the peaberry's popularity began with home roasters, who enjoyed its natural resistance to scorching as it rolled in the pan. It is similar in cup quality to the flat bean, though it demands a slightly higher price.

Indian

Legend attributes the first coffee trees in India to a Moslem pilgrim who smuggled seven seeds out of Mecca strapped to his belly around 1600. The real Indian coffee industry, however, got its start several centuries later— the creation of British colonial rulers who organized a plantation system and set up processing and export facilities. India's current coffee production tops off at about two million bags a year, more than half of that *arabica*. The United States gets about 20 percent of the coffee grown in India, the Soviet Union up to 40 percent.

Most of the coffees grown on the subcontinent are delicately winey and very rich, with Nilgiris from the state of Tamil Nadu and Tellicherry and Malabar from the state of Karala the most notable examples. However, a full 84 percent of the *arabica* grown in India comes from the state of Karnataka and goes out to the world under that region's former name, Mysore. Few coffee lovers go into trances over this heavy-bodied, mountain-grown coffee, yet there are those who admire its low acidity. The best advice is to blend Mysore with a highly acidic coffee in hopes of a happy compromise. Those with a preference for the mellowness promised by a Mysore would probably find that characteristic delivered more fully by coffee grown in Sumatra.

Sumatran Mandheling

Sumatra is another of those gigantic islands in the Malay Archipelago that go largely unnoticed on the global scene except when fine coffees are discussed. Java still gets votes from the old school and Celebes has enchanted many newcomers, yet the best coffees from Sumatra are ranked with the best in the world—without the corresponding prices of, for example, Jamaican Blue Mountain. Coffee cultivation got off to a strong start under the Dutch in the late 1600s, when Sumatra and its sister islands were known as the Netherlands Indies. The usual series of earthquakes and floods decimated the early crops, yet the colonial rulers persisted with fresh seedlings against the vagaries of Nature. From the early part of the nineteenth century up to 1908, coffee cultivation in Sumatra was carried out under Dutch government monopoly, except for a brief period of British control from 1811 to 1816. Under this system, natives were required to care for a specified number of coffee trees and turn over to the government for auction two-fifths of their cleaned and sorted beans. *Arabica* was virtually the only coffee grown in Sumatra until 1875, but a vicious attack of *Hemileia* convinced growers to replace it with hardy *robusta* below 3,000 feet and even with the strong but undesirable *Liberica*. Though most of Sumatra's coffee today is *robusta*, it is the surviving *arabica* that attracts connoisseurs. Crops are generally small, but Sumatra has an advantage over

Java in that its land is not coffee *moe*, or "coffee tired." Its principal growing districts lie along the southeast coast, but these play host only to *robusta*. The west coast, along which the coffee plant was first propagated here, remains the home of quality beans.

Both Mandheling and its only native rival, Ankola, are grown near the port of Padang in west-central Sumatra at altitudes of 2,500 to 5,000 feet. The highest priced coffee produced by the island, Mandheling as a bean is yellow to brown, depending on its ageing. The beans tend to be large and of a dull roast, yet they are wonderfully free of "quakers"—blighted or undeveloped individuals that detract from a coffee's quality in the cup. Mandheling is sometimes described as a coffee for fulfilled romantics, those who cherish a vision of wicker chairs under swaying palms at sunset as they sip. It is one of the most full-bodied coffees, grown with a richness that settles pleasurably into the corners of the mouth. This coffee possesses no more wineyness than it takes to be vibrant, and its flavor is smooth and full.

English coffee-house tiles

MILD, LIGHTER BODY

Connoisseurs often describe this category as closer to tea than coffee. That's how impressed or depressed they are by its thin body compared with either full-bodied grouping. These coffees are without doubt less pleasing to drinkers who seek a foodlike satisfaction from their brew, but they have a place for people who find a strong fermented taste overwhelming. If you like the flavor of winey coffees but reject their abruptness, this category offers what is in essence a subtle variation. Beyond that, it serves up by far the greatest diversity in taste, geographic origin and price, making it rich terrain for exploration.

Celebes Kalossi, Timor

Virtually all the coffee in Indonesia was wiped out by the attack of *Hemileia vastatrix* that also decimated the industries of Ceylon and India in 1878. It had almost regained its footing on the Malay Archipelago by the start of World War II, which knocked out cultivation all over again. Since the war ended, however, the region has sprung back to produce some of the finest coffees in the world. The island of Celebes is also known as Sulawesi, spreading like a hand with four fingers across the archipelago's midsection. Though the south of the isle produces an acceptable coffee called Rantepao, the name Celebes is most often found and indeed acclaimed in connection with Kalossi. This bean, which has become one of the world's most famous, flourishes on the southernmost finger, near the port of Manado.

Celebes coffee is a little hard to find, but most who manage agree it is worth the search. With a similar flavor to Mandheling coffee from nearby Sumatra, it is nonetheless more acidy and vibrant while surrendering something in richness and body. Celebes Kalossi shares these attributes with coffee from Timor, a Portuguese island across the Banda Sea to the south.

Costa Rican SHB

Nearly all Costa Rican coffee worthy of mention is grown in four districts surrounding the capital of San José —Tres Rios, Tarrazu, Heredia and Alajuela. Yet in this Central American nation, names count for less than numbers when coffee is being graded. The Pacific growths of Costa Rica are typed by the hardness of the bean, and that is determined by the altitude at which it is grown. "Strictly hard bean," abbreviated SHB, indicates coffee grown above 3,900 feet; followed by "good hard bean" or GHB at 3,300 to 3,900; "hard bean" at 2,600 to 3,300, and "medium hard bean" at 1,600 to 3,300, this last actually grown in a zone between the Pacific and Atlantic regions. Costa Rican coffees grown in the Atlantic areas carry that fact in their names, as in High Grown Atlantic. Because Costa Rican coffees are greatly admired by Europeans, the nation's total exports are tipped in that direction by as much as four to one. Though the American demand for Costa Rican coffees grows, the country continues to give its European customers a bit of special treatment, picking out imperfections from their coffees by hand while using machines for beans destined for the United States.

All coffees grown in Costa Rica are *arabica*, and nearly all are prepared for market by the wet method. SHB, by far the most distinguished produced by the land, uses an extremely bold to large bean to produce a coffee with high wineyness, fine body and good aroma. (Bold refers specifically to beans larger than good but smaller than large or extra large. Generically, bold can refer to any bean between good and extra large.) Some connoisseurs compare the total effect to that of a fine Burgundy. Though it would be a mistake to forget flavor amid all these names and numbers, it should be noted that not all Costa Rican is labeled correctly. A full 65 percent of the beans exported as Costa Rican are either SHB or the runner-up GHB, a fact that goes far in maintaining the country's reputation. However, the rest of the crop is less impressive, so asking questions about origins and methods at point of purchase will help sidestep disappointment.

Haitian

Haiti's coffee industry is among the most primitive in the Western Hemisphere, growing the beans on tiny peasant plots and processing them by makeshift variations on the world's two methods. Yet paradoxically, the industry operates under the weight of an amazingly detailed body of law—all aimed ostensibly at upgrading the quality of coffee bearing the Haitian name. In addition to the traditional wet and dry methods, some sections of the island nation use a third called triage, but this is generally considered unsatisfactory for the number of spoiled beans it produces. Most Haitian coffee is grown at 1,000 to 1,500 feet, on small holdings in the mountainous districts of St. Marc, Port-au-Prince, Petit Goâve, Jacmel, Cayes, Gonaives and Jérémie. Responding to its pervasive French influence, Haiti roasts its coffee dark for home consumption and ships most of its green beans across the Atlantic. France is joined by Italy, Belgium and the Netherlands in buying more than half the island's output, with the United States making off with another quarter.

Washed coffee from Haiti is a blue bean and tends to make an attractive roast, especially when handled in the French manner. Though only of average quality, it possesses a rich, fairly winey, somewhat sweet flavor that many coffee drinkers find appealing. This last quality can be attributed to heavy rainfall on the Haitian slopes as well as volcanic soil. The best of the government's numbing barrage of grades is "strictly high grown washed," which lets the sweetness come through nicely; the next is "high grown washed."

Hawaiian Kona

For all the coffee consumed in the United States, it grows only in one tiny section, far removed from the continent itself. The bean is cultivated in modest quantities on the slopes of the active volcano Mauna Loa on the island of Hawaii. Taking its name from the Kona district and thriving only beneath the snowfalls at 1,500 to 2,000 feet, this coffee enjoys some of the finest natural conditions found anywhere in the world. Holes must be dug with pick axes in order to plant in well-packed chunks of volcanic lava, and the plants' roots must be surrounded by soil from other parts of the island. Though nature provides gentle rainfall, sunny mornings, misty afternoons and shelter in the imposing form of Mauna Loa, fertilization must be provided throughout the year. These conditions, coupled with a miraculous absence of all disease, give the *arabica* grown on Hawaii the highest per-acre yield on earth—2,000 pounds compared with 500 to 800 in Latin America. The catch is that there are so few acres, just 3,600 in all, divided into 720 farms. Just over 20,000 bags a year are offered as whole bean, "all-purpose grind" and instant. Even this tiny annual yield is threatened by the higher profits to be made elsewhere in an economy inflated by tourism and a high cost of living. Children of the Japanese and Portuguese families that ran the coffee farms in this century are finding more enticing work and more satisfying paychecks in the service industries.

The future of Kona coffee may be as misty as Mauna Loa in the afternoon, but there is nothing uncertain about its quality. It remains a treasure when discovered in its fresh unblended form. A rich coffee with a mellow, straightforward flavor, Kona is medium bodied, fairly winey and overwhelmingly aromatic. It might be the coffee for you if you love tantalizing scents, find Indonesian grinds too rich, Africans too winey and Latin Americans too sharp—and if, of course, you can find it.

Jamaican Blue Mountain

An island nation that produces some of the world's least distinguished coffees in its lowlands looks to its heights for some of the most distinguished, not to mention most controversial and most expensive. The best Jamaican coffee is grown on a mountainous ridge that runs the length of the island from east to west. Each year, fewer than 1,000 barrels of Jamaican Blue Mountain coffee are produced on the Wallenford Estate, and nearly all of that is whisked away quickly for shipment to Japan. Elsewhere, this combination of rarity, quality and no small marketing genius account for top prices year after year. Considering the amount of money involved, the number of people trying to get some of it is not surprising. There is a heated controversy in the 7,000-foot Blue Mountains, and especially along the lower slopes, about what it takes to warrant the name. The people at the Wallenford Estate insist that only their coffee has that right, a claim supported by taste buds in far-flung if elitist corners of the globe. There are others, however, who insist Blue Mountain applies to any coffee grown in the district. The problem is not that these coffees are inferior, since all are similar to the Wallenford and many are quite satisfying. The problem is that some unscrupulous merchants will try to pass off coffee grown outside the district for Blue Mountain. Only 2 percent of the Blue Mountain crop is exported to the United States. Be especially careful that Blue Mountain allegedly brought back from Japan at great trouble and expense is not a considerably less revered Jamaican.

Level-headed coffee experts, who talk about the rich, heavy body of Sumatran Mandheling or the spicy tones of Guatemalan Antigua, tend to speak of true Blue Mountain only in terms of perfection. For the record, though, it is bluish-green when washed and makes a highly attractive roast, with beans free of defects and a uniformly bold size. Blue Mountain is extremely mellow, sweet tasting, and aromatic. This subtle balance of flavor and aroma, body and wineyness makes it nothing less than exquisite. Yet even if you are willing to pay the price but unable to find Blue Mountain, despair is not the only alternative. Maracaibo from Venezuela is a similar coffee, not to mention a classy one in its own right, as are Kona from Hawaii and the high-grown beans of Kenya, Tanzania and Cameroon. Other Jamaican coffees are also a possibility. These, sold as Jamaican High Mountain or Blue Mountain Type Jamaican, should be tasted before they are purchased.

Java

At one time, the island of Java in Indonesia produced more coffee than any other place in the world. Its domination of the market, with deliveries throughout the world via wooden sailing ships as early as 1706, made its name synonymous with coffee everywhere. The Dutch planted the first *arabica* trees there early in coffee history, but the rust disease in 1878 and World War II took care of most of those. Even though disease-resistant *robusta* was chosen to replace the lost trees, *arabica* has made a mild comeback. It's against the law to sell *robusta* as Java coffee, but consumers are warned to be wary nonetheless. *Arabica* growths from other Indonesian islands—Sumatra, Celebes, Bali and Flores—are sometimes sold under the name Java in a practice dating back to 1712. The only real confusion, however, is with the otherwise respectable "Java" from El Salvador. True Java crops are relatively small, as is true with most other *arabica* across Indonesia. But they are available in the United States.

Bearing a smaller bean than most coffees from Sumatra and finding less favor with many buyers, Java often features an unpleasantly grassy flavor when drunk unblended with other types. At its best, however, it is full-bodied and rich, with more wineyness than Celebes or Sumatran, plus the slightest smokiness or spice. It is wonderfully sturdy and direct, one of the world's landmark coffees. Traditionally, the best Javas hail from Preanger, Cheribon and Batavia.

Mexican Altura, Maragogipe

Some Americans buying Mexican coffee and brewing it in their homes are disappointed when it has little in common with the strong black beverage they enjoyed in travels through the hinterland. That, however, is made almost exclusively from cheaper beans unworthy of export—dark roasted and glazed with sugar. The only hope for a nostalgic taste of such coffee lies in cans from the southern United States and grinds sold in Puerto Rican, Cuban or Mexican markets. The finest Mexican exports are a very different story. Nearly all are grown in the south of Mexico, in the states of Oaxaca west of the central mountain range and Veracruz to the east. Coffees produced by estates in Veracruz, especially the high-grown Altura Coatepec, are the greatest coming out of Mexico. Other noteworthy Alturas from the state are the Orizaba and Huatusco. Altura is the best grade of coffee exported by Mexico, followed by *prima lavada* (prime washed) and *buena lavada* (good washed). In recent years, the country has almost tripled its annual yield, raising it to three million bags. Yet half the coffee produced there is consumed by Mexicans themselves, inspired perhaps by promotions mounted by the Mexican Coffee Institute.

Because it comes from a wide-ranging area, Mexican coffees can vary dramatically in quality and taste, more so than Guatemalan or Costa Rican yet less than Brazilian. In general, even the best lack the richness and body of the world's great coffees. Yet they possess a delicacy many find reminiscent of light white wine, with the added interest of a dry, acidy snap. Mexican is a good choice for people who like their coffee black but lighter than the syrupy brews of Arabia. As for a type of Mexican coffee called Maragogipe, assessments vary wildly. It is actually a variety of *arabica* that produces a large, rather porous bean. Though it has spread all over the world following a spontaneous appearance near the town of Maragogipe in Brazil, it has failed to impress most experts with its "woody and disagreeable" taste. A few defend it passionately, however, pointing out that in Mexico and elsewhere it sports a heavier, more satisfying body than other *arabica* from the same region.

Peruvian

Considered nearly worthless coffee as late as the 1930s, Peruvian today is a comer. All the coffees produced there are *arabica*, and all are sold under a single national designation. The beans range from medium to bold in size, from bluish to yellow in hue. The United States purchases more than half Peru's annual export, which tops 800,000 bags and appears to be growing after a very slow start. Forty percent of the total crop comes from the central Chanchamayo Valley, but the finest growths come from the 3,000- to 5,000-foot Andes in the northern part of the country. This area is the most likely source for the Peruvian coffee found in American specialty stores. Most of Peru's crop is grown on agricultural cooperatives, while the government applies a strong hand to promotion of the nation's coffee.

Modern-day coffee drinkers do not share the prejudice against Peruvian of an earlier generation. Today's drinkers are encouraged by improvements in quality and consistency pushed forward by the government; thin-bodied but flavorful, coffee from Peru generally resembles some of the lesser growths from Veracruz in Mexico. Regional marks worth noting are those indicating the northern, high-grown varieties: Piura, Lambayeque, San Martín and Cajamarca.

Salvador High Grown

El Salvador grows virtually nothing but coffee, so it's a shame more of it isn't better. All the same, the finest growths from this mountainous Central American nation have found admirers here and there—enough to keep growers in business in all the country's 14 counties. All *arabica* and 94 percent washed, Salvadors are cultivated on a central volcanic range from 1,500 to 5,000 feet. They account for just under 5 percent of the world's total export, with West Germany the nation's best customer. The United States purchases half a million bags a year, most of that entering through San Francisco.

Often termed the equal of Guatemalan coffees, Salvadors are similarly classed by altitude rather than growing region or shipping port. The best 15 percent of the crop is designated "central strictly high grown" and 55 percent "central standard." Though not particularly flavorful or aromatic, beans of the top two grades are appreciated nonetheless for their good acidity and body. The Salvadors found in the United States are nearly always of the inferior "central standard" classification grown below 3,000 feet. Slight in body, they have a nice acidity and a pleasantly winey taste.

Venezuelan

The size of Venezuela's coffee crop has remained fairly steady over the past decade, but increasing consumption by the natives has cut significantly into the beans available for export. Venezuelans consume more than half the million bags their homeland produces each year, with the United States getting up to two-thirds of the beans that make it into export. Though Venezuela once challenged Colombia on the world coffee market, the discovery of "black gold" pushed the brown bean into relative unimportance to the total economy. The country now turns out less than 1 percent of the coffee served around the world. Beans grown in Venezuela are classified as Maracaibo, Caracas and Puerto Cabello—the first and last taking the name of their shipping ports. The other group, named after the nation's capital, is shipped through nearby La Guaira. Each notation can be subdivided further by the districts in which its principal plantations lie. Coffee farms are found at levels from 1,000 to 5,000 feet, with the better coffees generally hailing from the higher altitudes.

Many coffee lovers reserve Venezuelan types for blending, with a clear preference for mixing them with French and Italian roasts. Others, however, have developed a taste for any or all of the regional distinctions most evident when drunk single bean. Caracas growths are generally light and winey, with a peculiar flavor that many an educated palate finds pleasing. At equal prices, they even get the nod over Colombian Bogotás, since they exhibit more body in the cup. Puerto Cabello coffees are rated just below Caracas, grown at a lower altitude and correspondingly inferior in flavor. Táchira and Mérida coffees are considered the best of the Maracaibo. They tend toward sharp acidity when new, but mellow and take on body with age.

Metal token from Andrew Vincent's coffee house in Friday Street, London. In the seventeenth-century, tokens of small value were issued by ordinary citizens for use by their neighbors. In this case the token was from a coffee house.

Leather threepenny token from Robins coffee house in Old Jewry

A Guide-at-a-Glance
to Coffee Beans

Brazil
MARKET NAMES: Bourbon Santos (Santos Bourbon), Sul de Minas.

HIGHEST CLASSIFICATION: Brazils are classified according to the quality of their drink; strictly soft bean is the best.

FLAVOR: Dry, heavy body, sweet.

Colombia
MARKET NAMES: Best known are Medellín and Armenia; numerous others.

HIGHEST CLASSIFICATION: Supremo; excelso.

FLAVOR: Winey, heavy body, aromatic.

Costa Rica
MARKET NAMES: Strictly Hard Bean (SHB), Tres Rios, Tarrazu, Cartago, San José, Curridabat, San Ramon, Heredia, Montes de Oca, Naranja, Sabonilla.

HIGHEST CLASSIFICATION: Strictly hard bean.

FLAVOR: Winey, medium body, very aromatic.

Dominican Republic
MARKET NAMES: Generally known as Santo Domingo; also may include the producer's name or trade name or registered trademark.

HIGHEST CLASSIFICATION: None.

FLAVOR: Little wineyness, very light body.

Ecuador
MARKET NAME: Ecuadors.

HIGHEST CLASSIFICATION: Unico, large bean, hand picked.

FLAVOR: Slight wineyness, light body, somewhat woody.

El Salvador
MARKET NAME: Salvador; may also include the producer or exporter of shipment.
HIGHEST CLASSIFICATION: Strictly high grown.
FLAVOR: Winey, medium body, mild taste, aromatic.

Ethiopia
MARKET NAMES: Djimmah, Wild Ethiopian; Sidamo, also Wild Ethiopian; Harar, Plantation Grown.
HIGHEST CLASSIFICATION: Djimmah and Sidamo No. 5; Harar Longberry.
FLAVOR: Very winey, heavy body, very aromatic.

Guatemala
MARKET NAMES: Numerous appellations based on production district and the planter or exporter; best known are Cobán and Antigua.
HIGHEST CLASSIFICATION: Strictly high-grown central, strictly hard bean.
FLAVOR: Extremely winey, heavy body, very aromatic.

Haiti
MARKET NAMES: Washed Strictly High Grown; others of lesser quality.
HIGHEST CLASSIFICATION: Large bean; XXXXX OR XXXX.
FLAVOR: Somewhat musty or woody, very dry, strong taste.

Hawaii
MARKET NAME: Kona.
HIGHEST CLASSIFICATION: Extra fancy.
FLAVOR: Mild wineyness, light body.

Honduras
MARKET NAME: Washed Honduras.
HIGHEST CLASSIFICATION: High-grown.
FLAVOR: Mildly winey, light body, mild taste.

India
MARKET NAME: Malabar.
HIGHEST CLASSIFICATION: Unwashed, Malabar AA Monsoon.
FLAVOR: Dry, mild to heavy body, aromatic.

India, continued
MARKET NAMES: Mysore, Babadudan.
HIGHEST CLASSIFICATION: Washed *arabica*, Plantation A.
FLAVOR: Winey, heavy to medium body, aromatic.

Indonesia
MARKET NAMES: Sumatran, Mandheling.
HIGHEST CLASSIFICATION: None.
FLAVOR: Dry, heavy body.

MARKET NAMES: Java, Celebes, Kalossi, Bali, Flores, and
    Timor.
HIGHEST CLASSIFICATION: None.
FLAVOR: Slightly winey, medium body.

Jamaica
MARKET NAMES: Jamaican Blue Mountain, Jamaican High
    Mountain, Supreme, Prime Jamaican Washed.
HIGHEST CLASSIFICATION: None.
FLAVOR: Mind wineyness, light body, very aromatic.

Kenya
MARKET NAME: Kenya AA.
HIGHEST CLASSIFICATION: AA, extra large bean.
FLAVOR: Extremely winey, heavy body, aromatic.

Mexico
MARKET NAMES: Altura Coatepec, Altura Pluma, Altura
    Oaxaca.
HIGHEST CLASSIFICATION: Altura (high-grown).
FLAVOR: Mild wineyness, light body, aromatic.

Nicaragua
MARKET NAMES: Jinotega, Matagalpas, Washed Nicara-
    guan.
HIGHEST CLASSIFICATION: Strictly high-grown central.
FLAVOR: Mild wineyness, light body, aromatic.

Panama
MARKET NAME: Panama.
HIGHEST CLASSIFICATION: None.
FLAVOR: Mild wineyness, medium body, aromatic.

Peru

MARKET NAMES: Puira, Lambayeque, San Martin, Caja-
marca.
HIGHEST CLASSIFICATION: None.
FLAVOR: Fairly winey, medium body, aromatic.

Tanzania

MARKET NAME: Tanzanian AA.
HIGHEST CLASSIFICATION: AA, extra large bean.
FLAVOR: Extremely winey, heavy body, aromatic.

Venezuela

MARKET NAMES: Best known is Maracaibo; numerous oth-
ers.
HIGHEST CLASSIFICATION: Large bean, superior.
FLAVOR: Mild wineyness, medium body, aromatic.

Yemen

MARKET NAMES: Yemen Mocha, Mattari Mocha, Sharki
Mocha, Sanani Mocha.
HIGHEST CLASSIFICATION: None.
FLAVOR: Winey, heavy body, mildly aromatic.

Zaire

MARKET NAME: Zaire *arabica*.
HIGHEST CLASSIFICATION: Nos. 1 to 3, fine quality.
FLAVOR: Winey, medium body, aromatic.

A Word on Tasting

This quick tour of the world's finest coffees
must end as it began, with your taste buds. The descriptions of these famous brews, whether euphoric or highly
uncomplimentary, stand only as means to an end. And
the system of grouping them, while based on solid chemistry, is intended only to help your preferences find for-
mat, your feelings find voice. Beyond these snippets of
history and geography, angels and fools alike should tread
cautiously.
The more coffees you have tasted, the greater your sensitivity to both their striking and subtle contrasts. So the

COFFEE HOUSE JESTS

Before the Revolution, coffee houses were not, as a rule, frequented by persons of highest rank. The Restoration changed that. They became fashionable and even places to transact state business. From a 1688 edition of Coffee House Jests.

secret is to taste coffees at every turn, as many and as often as possible. Many shops let you sample their selections in brewed form, and if you are lucky the choices will change regularly until you know your way around.

Yet it takes a bit of effort. Despite the similarities of coffee appreciation to that of wine, it is highly unlikely you will be invited anytime soon to a chic coffee tasting or a commercial sip-around to celebrate the latest crop's arrival. Therefore you must take the samples when they are offered and make your own surveys when they are not. Start with the introduction given here, pull together a few guidelines based on your established preferences and proceed.

Buy a different coffee each week, or perhaps a different coffee each month. Buy a specialty coffee to taste in the evenings, while keeping Old Faithful to build your mornings around. This is a quest, not a college course, and the adventures along the way can be as pleasurable as finding the ultimate cup.

About Decaffeinated Coffee

For the longest time, lovers of gourmet coffees turned up their noses (and turned down their cups) when offered a brew that was decaffeinated. If they could not enjoy the full flavor and body they relished, many insisted it was not worth drinking at all. And they had every reason to feel this way. Primitive methods of removing caffeine deprived coffee of many of its finer qualities, making its consumption at best a boring, frustrating compromise.

A growing market for good decaf was there, however. The industry's technological wizards have worked nonstop for twenty years to produce a brew that meets the standards of flavor and body that connoisseurs have come to demand. Their creation still might not suit everyone's taste. Indeed, most coffee experts see no reason to drink decaf without a push from the doctor to address some specific health issue. The good news is that if push does come to shove, decaffeinated coffees are available in the volume and variety—and most of all, the quality—that make them valid additions to the gourmet coffee scene.

The numbers can be impressive. The International Coffee Organization, in its most recent survey of the beverage in the United States, discovered that a full 21 percent of the coffee consumed is decaffeinated—five times the proportion the ICO found when it first started measuring such things in 1961. The organization cites several reasons for the change, primarily an aging population seeking to limit its use of various caffeine-containing products and an increased awareness of decaffeinated coffees on the market.

Interestingly, the growth of decaf comes at a time of heightened anxiety about food products using additives or undergoing extensive processing between their natural and store-bought states. The coffee industry has developed two basic processes that present no measurable health risk. Caffeine can be removed either by the water or solvent process. In either case, the amount of residue left by the decaffeinating agent is extremely minute. All substances used in the process are commonly employed in the food industry, and all methods are subject to regulations set down by the Food and Drug Administration.

Scientifically speaking, caffeine is the single component in coffee that persists throughout the deep-seated series of changes caused by the roasting process. It is the single most characteristic ingredient in coffee, the one that confers upon the beverage its special stimulating qualities. Also found in tea, in maté and to some extent in cocoa, caffeine occurs not only in the coffee bean but also in smaller quantities in the flowers, the leaves, the small stems, and in the pulp of the berry surrounding the seed. In its free and pure state, it forms slender white, needle-shaped crystals that give off a silky luster. When crystallized from solution, caffeine tends to form clusters that strike many as attractive.

The average cup of coffee contains between one and two grains of caffeine. Researchers say that while this amount can produce a quicker heartbeat, greater mental activity and difficulty sleeping in some people, four or five times as much will have no effect on others. In the use of a beverage such as coffee, individual tolerance as well as individual taste must be accommodated. Many studies linking the caffeine in coffee to a wide variety of human woes, from impatience to sterility, have been based on consumption of up to fifty cups a day.

All the same, for those bothered by caffeine, the two basic methods of extraction are water and solvent, with each variation employing a two-step process. It is a good idea, not to mention an interesting investigation, to discuss these methods with your gourmet coffee dealer and determine which is used in the decaffeinated beans he sells.

Extraction by water. The first water method is the one used most widely in the United States. Unroasted beans are soaked for hours in a mixture of water and coffee components so that 97 percent of the caffeine is removed. The components help prevent substances other than caffeine from leaching out, while helping to preserve flavor and aroma in the finished product. The caffeine-rich mixture is then drained from the beans, which are dried, roasted and processed. The mixture itself is transferred to a separate section of the plant to be combined with methylene chloride, which draws out the caffeine. The methylene chloride and the caffeine are both removed by steaming, leaving the mixture ready to work on subsequent batches of beans.

H_2O

There is a second method of extraction by water, often called the "Swiss Water Process." Though the method varies from place to place, it usually involves immersing unroasted coffee beans in a water solution that removes about 97 percent of the caffeine along with those coffee components readily dissolved in water. This mixture then is drained from the beans and filtered through vessels containing activated charcoal that has been preheated with sucrose and formic acid. As the mixture passes through the vessels, caffeine is removed by the charcoal. Because this charcoal has been treated, the amount of coffee components that would otherwise be retained is reduced. At this point, the essentially caffeine-free mixture drawn from the vessels is concentrated and added to the partially dried beans, making them ready for drying and roasting.

H_2O

Extraction by solvent. Solvent speeds up the decaffeination process and, as a consequence, disturbs fewer of the desirable coffee components while minimizing cost. The first of four methods in this category and the most widely used employs methylene chloride. First, the green, unroasted beans are steamed to soften them and soaked in a methylene chloride solution which absorbs the caffeine. The beans are then heated and blown with steam until

SOLVENT

the solution has evaporated. This process is repeated until 97 percent or more of the caffeine has been removed.

The methylene chloride methods is quick, easy and, according to the Food and Drug Administration, safe. Only a minute amount of the solvent (less than one part per million) may make it all the way to your cup. This is one-tenth the amount the FDA considers safe, and because coffee is roasted at high temperatures and methylene chloride evaporates easily, it is doubtful you'll end up ingesting any at all.

SOLVENT The second method in this category, a process using ethyl acetate, is used in the United States most often to produce dehydrated instant coffees. Yet it may also be used for some ground coffees. In this sequence of treatments, the ethyl acetate removes caffeine and other components directly from liquid coffee that will be processed further to make instant. The caffeine-bearing mixture is separated from the coffee and concentrated by evaporation, then it is mixed with water to remove the caffeine and some of the coffee components. The caffeine-free ethyl acetate, still carrying most of the components, is then combined with the remaining liquid coffee. The solvent is removed by evaporation and can be used again. The caffeine-rich water is concentrated, and the caffeine is solidified and removed. The water, still containing much of the dissolved coffee components, can be used to produce another batch of liquid coffee.

In this category's third method, carbon dioxide is used as a decaffeination solvent on a limited basis in Europe, although some coffee processed this way is appearing in the United States as well. The CO_2 is used under high pressure to decaffeinate unroasted beans, which are then transferred to an extraction vessel to which pressurized CO_2 and water are added. The contents are kept under high pressure for several hours, then the beans are separated from the CO_2 and the water. The beans are subsequently dried, roasted and packaged, while the caffeine is recovered from the pressurized CO_2 either by filtration through wet charcoal or by evaporation. In either case, the CO_2 is collected and used to decaffeinate more coffee.

The fourth method for extraction by solvent uses a

group of compounds called triglycerides that are found naturally in coffee oil. The oil may be obtained from coffee grounds in either of two ways—simply pressed out or extracted with hexane, which afterward is evaporated out of the oil, recovered and used again. Coffee oil usually is used to decaffeinate green beans, but it can also be used directly on roasted coffee or on an extract of roasted coffee. The beans are placed in a vessel where coffee oil flows through them for several hours at high temperature, removing 97 percent of the caffeine. The caffeine is recovered, while the oil is purified to use again.

"The French Coffee House" by Thomas Rowlandson

Outfitting the Coffee Gourmet

*Y*OU don't need much equipment to make coffee, but you do need something—unless munching on unroasted beans is your idea of a great time. Over the years a dizzying array of paraphernalia has evolved, with the choices only getting more numerous and intimidating with the recent onset of chic. It's time to simplify and quantify, to decide how much of what's offered is right for you and how much is hokum at best. The thing you'll need most is a coffee pot, so this assessment begins with a look at just how coffee can be made and nine applications of these basic methods. Then there's the matter of home grinding and roasting, complete with the joys and sorrows of each, a glance at gourmet accessories currently on the market and a final note on coffee antiques.

Coffee Pot Wisdom

The search for a coffee pot begins with a simple fact. There are only two ways of extracting the flavor you know and love from coffee beans. The oldest is decoction, boiling a substance until its flavor is taken out. Used as a medicine as early as 1000 A.D., coffee appeared as a decoction of dried fruit, beans and hulls. Within two centuries, the decoction was made with the dried hulls alone, and it evolved over the next two centuries through whole roasted beans to ground roasted coffee. The second basic method, infusion, is extraction accomplished at any temperature below boiling. It can be broken down into several categories: steeping, percolation (dripping) and filtration. In steeping, the simplest form, hot water is mixed with ground coffee. That's it. Percolation actually means dripping the water through fine apertures in china or metal, though the name has been perverted by the modern pump percolator. And filtration is dripping through a porous substance such as cloth or paper.

There is no real magic to choosing a coffee pot. With the exception of a decision based purely on looks, or one based solely on price, the search is less a major statement of theme than a collection of small advantages. Common

George II silver Lighthouse coffee pot, 1729

sense should sit at the forefront of your judgment during any coffee pot shopping trip, leaving metaphysics out.

Your pot, for example, should be easy to clean. The oils released in the brewing process form an almost invisible film that will turn rancid and contaminate future brews unless removed with a mild detergent or baking soda. A metal pot, whatever its appeal, must be assessed in light of its tendency to cause bitterness or astringency or absorb old flavors. Glass and porcelain are the best materials, followed in order by stainless steel, nickel, copper, aluminum and tin plate.

Most important is the pot's brewing cycle and ability to maintain this time sequence accurately. Depending on the amount of coffee you're brewing, a pump percolator should take six to eight minutes, a drip or filter pot four to six and a vacuum pot one to four.

Only within these recommended limitations can the disastrous effects of over- or underextraction be avoided. It's that simple, and unless your pot can consistently operate accordingly, it's not the one for you. A pot also must be able to operate successfully within its stated cup capacities. If it promises two to four cups of coffee, it must do two as well as four, the same if it promises four to eight. Decide how much coffee you need at a single sitting (in general, reheated coffee should be snubbed), find a coffee maker suited to that amount and make sure it fills the bill.

Finally, your choice of coffee pot might reflect a strong preference for a certain type of brew. Drinkers who love only Turkish coffee would do well to simply track down an *ibrik* in which to brew it. Devotees of espresso might purchase a pressurized Italian gadget and live happily ever after. For most people, though—and especially for those with an eye toward experiencing the variety coffee has to offer—there are no such easy answers. So find a pot that does what it promises and does it well every time. The rest, happily, is up to you.

Open Pot

This is a far cry from the best way to make coffee, but it is certainly the oldest and probably the simplest. It has several variations, from the ridiculous hobo coffee to the sublime Turkish coffee. Boiling, of course, is a method as old as herdsman Kaldi, whose interest in coffee was sparked by his happy, bean-munching goats. Steeping, the earliest form of infusion, was introduced into France in 1711. Within half a century, it was used by almost everyone there, even though Americans were still boiling whole roasted beans.

Time-tested is the key to whatever appeal the open pot method might have—the Arab decoction was the only game in town for 400 years. Many people continue to like the strong and bitter brew produced by boiling in a Turkish ibrik, a tall, long-handled copper or brass pot that has no cover and tapers toward the top. It carries an image both exotic and macho. Boiled coffee, however, tends to be cloudy, even when clarified, lacking in aromatic oils and extra high in caffeine concentration. Steeping remains nearly foolproof, since any grind of coffee will do and no special pot is necessary. A mellow, aromatic cup results, one that's stronger than drip yet less bitter than percolated. Today, steeping finds its largest group of supporters in Scandinavia, which prides itself on fine coffee. Swedes use all sorts of devices to steep their brew, from a copper pot with a wooden handle designed to stand in the coals to a glass-globe pot for stove use, which is enclosed in a felt-lined brass cozy.

On the negative side, steeped coffee becomes bitter from overextraction if the grounds are not removed immediately after brewing. And it is difficult to keep the grounds out of your cup, however carefully you may pour. Decanting the coffee into a serving pot is often the best remedy for this.

To make Turkish coffee for two, use a traditional long-handled ibrik or small saucepan and one heaping teaspoon of finely ground Turkish coffee. Pour 1½ demitasses (3 ounces) of water into the pan, add two generous teaspoons of sugar and bring to a boil. Stir in the coffee and boil up three times before removing from the fire. Add a little cold water. Serve the froth first, then carefully pour or spoon the thick brew into the cups.

Steeping begins with the correct amount of cold, fresh water brought to a boil in a pot, kettle or pail. Remove this from the heat, add ground coffee, stir and cover pot for steeping. This should take two to four minutes for fine grind, six to eight minutes for coarse. Just before serving, add a small amount of cold water to settle the grounds, then pour through a cloth or wire strainer into cups or a warmed serving pot.

To boil coffee the old-fashioned way favored, or at least tolerated by the pioneers, bring water to a boil in a coffee pot or kettle, add coarse ground coffee and boil for 5 minutes or more. Cold water can be added to settle the grounds, though other tried and true clarifiers include eggshells, egg whites, fish skin and salt pork rind.

French Plunger Pot

A bit of mechanical ingenuity enters the picture here, raising the steeping process to something between an art and an applied science. The plunger involves letting coffee steep in freshly boiled water inside a glass cylinder, then pressing down on a mechanism to separate brew from grounds. A pot of this type, which is better suited to French-roast coffee than American, will retail for around $68 for the Melior at the upper end, down to about $25 for the Bodum.

The French plunger produces strong hot coffee in a hurry. The Melior in particular is an attractive device that makes it possible to brew coffee right at the table. There is a built-in steel screen for more convenience than steeping in an open pot. Among the drawbacks, the coffee grounds stay at the bottom until the entire pot is served, increasing the chances of bitterness, and if you let the coffee steep initially as long as it really should, the brew tends to be lukewarm by the time it is poured. The pot is not the sort you can set on a warming unit.

All-purpose or drip grind coffee should be measured into the plunger's tall, heat-resistant glass cylinder. Add the correct amount of boiling water and let steep up to five minutes. Push down the plunger with its perforated metal disc and fine fire screen until it traps coffee grounds at the bottom. Pour from the cylinder and serve. The longer you wait to plunge, the stronger the brew will be.

Drip Pot

In kitchens around New Orleans, this is the favored method for brewing coffee destined to become traditional café au lait. Though hardly a percolator in the usual American sense, it uses a form of percolation—passing hot water through ground coffee and then through small holes into the pot below. Historically, dripping coffee followed boiling and steeping. It owes its invention to the Archbishop of Paris, Jean Baptiste de Belloy, and its development to Benjamin Thompson of Woburn, Massachusetts—a bizarre figure more often referred to as Count Rumford. Besides introducing cream and sugar to coffee, the count earned a place in history for a device that kept the grounds compressed in their container, preventing them from agitation by the water. In its standard form today, the pot is a three-piece aluminum or stainless steel device: a water receiver, a coffee basket and a beverage receiver. The best aluminum drip pot is the Drip-O-Lator, usually priced from $10.50 for a three-cup version to $13 for the nine cup. A favorite among New Orleans residents and visitors (and a popular souvenir) is the porcelain French *biggin*, which produces a thick brew with an intensity rivaling espresso's. A two-cup biggin can be had for about $24.50; the four-cup for $29.50.

When thoroughly washed before first use and after extended inactivity, aluminum drip pots produce a flavorful cup without bitterness. The porcelain variation is free of even the threat of metallic aftertaste, and both make strong coffee with relatively few grounds. The permanent porcelain filter also saves money on paper filters, since none are needed. This pot is an elegant accessory that can even double for tea making. It should not, however, be placed over direct heat (a heating pad is a must), and the porcelain filter is generally less effective at straining off grounds than either paper or cloth. Finally, this drip method is time-consuming and troublesome, since boiling water must be added at intervals to produce the proper drip.

Pour water that has just come to a boil through the water dispenser onto drip grind coffee in the removable section with a filter bottom. The serving pot should be preheated to receive and pamper the thick, black brew.

Neapolitan Filter Drip

The bracing Italian brew called espresso has made great inroads of late as a favorite of American coffee drinkers, yet the machinery needed to produce espresso remains more troublesome or expensive than many will tolerate. If you fall into this category, you might consider the Neapolitan. It is officially known as the *machinetta*, though it is sometimes referred to as the "upside-down pot" because you turn it over to send boiling water flowing through the coffee. This pot consists of two cylinders—one with a spout and one without—and a two-piece coffee basket that fits between them. Experts, of course, are quick to point out that no coffee made without steam and pressure can be as strong or heavy-bodied as espresso. But the Neapolitan filter drip does a fine job of brewing dark Italian coffee, as well as a French variation known as *café filtre*.

The *machinetta* turns out strong coffee with only a limited amount of sediment, and it comes in models small enough to make just two cups successfully—without having to underutilize the pot's capacity to the coffee's detriment. The limitations, however, are considerable. It is no small achievement to flip the hot machinetta over, even using both hands and heatproof plastic handles. There is always the small chance that the inevitable dribble of water means the entire unit is about to separate, sending burning coffee and waterlogged grounds over the counter or tabletop. Finally, since most Neapolitan units are made of aluminum, there can be a metallic aftertaste to the coffee. Your only hope of avoiding this is to give the pot a thorough cleaning after each and every use.

Pour cold water into the spoutless boiler and slip in the filter basket sleeve. Add coffee and screw on the perforated lid, then set the spouted container on top and the entire unit on the heat. When the water is hot enough to spurt from the tiny hole at the top of the boiler, remove the entire outfit from the heat, invert the pot and allow the water to trickle through the coffee into the pouring section. Remove the boiler and filter sleeve, place the lid on the serving unit and pour. Like espresso, coffee prepared in a Neapolitan filter drip should be served in demitasse cups or wine glasses; a twist of lemon peel and sugar are optional but cream is never acceptable.

Filter Drip Cone

At its simplest, filter drip coffee can be made literally by hand. The Brazilians do it every day to produce their tiny, steaming cups of *cafezinho*. They measure dark roasted, finely ground coffee into a cloth strainer or cafezinho bag, pour in boiling water and hold the entire thing over a pot until all the water has run through. Cafezinho should be served sweetened in demitasse cups. There are, all the same, several variations on this Brazilian favorite, most using machinery that attaches the filter to the pot. The basic set-up includes a pot or carafe of metal or Pyrex and a paper filter held in place above its aperture. Among the popular cone-shaped filter systems are the Tricolette, Chemex and David Douglas; the Melitta system using a flat-bottomed filter is quickest and most efficient. The 6-cup Melitta runs $10.99, while the 8-cup Chemex carries a price tag of $21.95.

Filter drip is considered the most effective method for producing mellow coffee free of oils and even the finest sediment, thanks to the paper filters. It is also possible that you will be able to produce a brew to your liking using less than two tablespoons of coffee per cup. The filter drip cone is easy to clean, since all the grounds can be spirited away in their soggy paper. Several sizes of inexpensive filter holders are available. As for the negatives, there is the cost of the filters, which need replacing after each use. The filter drip unit also might be hard to hold if it lacks a handle and tends to cool down before you are ready for it to do so, making a serving warmer a justifiable investment.

Rinse the pot out with hot water to preheat, then set the filter in the cone and add drip grind coffee. Pour about half the measured boiling water into the filter and stir well to make sure all the grounds get wet; let this drip through and add the rest of the water. When all the water has dripped through, remove the cone, stir the brewed coffee and serve.

Electric Drip Filter

Coffee lovers are heartened by the growing popularity of these devices, since they seem destined by their ease and economy to replace the pump percolator as America's coffee maker. Beyond the home kitchen, where their push-button convenience, easily followed directions and automatic time settings are a major plus, electric drip pots have in recent years improved (or at least standardized) the quality of coffee served in restaurants and even that last bastion of battery acid, the American office. Coffee makers bearing the names Melitta, Krups, West Bend, Braun, General Electric, Mr. Coffee, Bunn and Norelco apply a sort of thoughtless automation to the old-fashioned filter process—the coffee maker regulates the brewing cycle for you. As long as you use the right amount of coffee and the right amount of water, it's very hard to miss. The price range here is rather large, from $22 to $95. One of the best is the Brewmaster by Krups for $80.

At least one device, the My Café by Toshiba, grinds as well as brews coffee. Its main selling point, of course, is convenience, since you only have to put in the correct amounts of beans and water and wait for your brew. The device can be programmed to start at certain times, and two water-flow systems allow control of the coffee's strength. The main limitation of the combination grinder/coffeemaker is that it uses a blade instead of a mill grinder, and so has less precision.

Electric drip filter systems are easy to operate and clean. They consistently make a good, clear brew and can turn out up to a cup a minute if pushed. They are faster and simpler than the old pump percolators, and light-years ahead in coffee quality. Most models shut off the unit that heats the water at the end of the brewing cycle and switch on a warming plate beneath the carafe to maintain the correct serving temperature. These units are less likely to tip over than percolators, since they have considerably larger bases. And the used filters are easy to remove and throw away.

Many drip coffee brewers, both electric and nonelectric, can now be used with permanent filters. These filters are made of plastic or metal (often gold-plated) and work exactly like their paper counterparts except that they are washed instead of discarded after each use. Although a bit less convenient, permanent filters produce a more full-bodied cup because they allow important flavor components, which are trapped by paper filters, to pass into the final brew.

The electric filter drip method does have its limitations. Some models are unable to deliver flavorful coffee when operating at less than full capacity—especially when used to make only one or two cups. Also, automatic coffee makers are ill-disposed to individualists who prefer their brew stronger or weaker than the machine is designed to produce. Grind and proportion can be adjusted, though overextraction might result from too fine a grind and underextraction from one that's too coarse. Since engineers are always tinkering with these things, you should assess the design and construction of any coffee maker that you consider buying. Be on the lookout for flimsy materials, hard-to-read markings and overly-complicated operations.

Place a paper or permanent filter of the proper size and shape in the filter basket (unless you have a permanent metal or plastic filter). Measure the proper amount of coffee into the basket and place it in position under the heated water outlet. Set the beverage receiver under the basket on the warming plate. Pour freshly drawn cold water into the tank, plug in and turn on. When the brewing is finished, stir the coffee and serve.

Vacuum Siphon

This system of making coffee should appeal to frustrated chemistry majors, since it looks more like an experiment than a kitchen device. The first fully developed vacuum system was perfected in 1840 by Robert Napier. This Scottish marine engineer's contribution to coffee science consisted of a silver globe, a mixing container, a siphon and a strainer. To produce a cup or two of brew, Napier placed a small amount of water in the globe and heated it with a gas burner. At the same time, he added boiling water to dry ground coffee in the mixing container, producing pressure in the globe that forced steam through the tube into the coffee mixture. Lowering the flame caused this steam to condense and form a vacuum that would pull brewed coffee back through the tube. The design is not very popular anymore, but a modern variation made by Bodum and sold for $19 does have a following. For all the complexity, it does turn out good coffee.

Coffee brewed by a vacuum siphon is free of sediment and retains much of its natural flavor and aroma, this last because there is only the slightest exposure to oxygen. The water contacts all the coffee rapidly and separates brew from grounds through a filter. The heat-resistant coffee server also can be used as a kettle to boil water for tea and other purposes. Among the vacuum siphon's limitations is the difficulty of removing the hot upper bowl after brewing. The tight rubber gasket works against you here, as does the absence of a handle, which is almost always the case. The unit must also be watched rather carefully when in operation, since it has no safety valves or automatic controls and could actually implode under pressure. It must be removed from the heat as soon as all the water has been forced by steam into the upper bowl. The glass siphon stopper is easily broken, and a warming plate is a must for keeping coffee hot until serving time.

Fortunately for Robert Napier's legacy, the how-to is much simpler than the how-does. Remove the upper bowl, insert a cloth or paper filter and add the proper amount of fine ground coffee. In the lower bowl, bring a measured amount of cold water to a boil and remove from the heat. Insert the top bowl tightly and return to reduced heat. Allow the water to rise and mix with coffee for one minute, stirring slightly. Remove the whole unit from the heat so the brewed coffee can return to the lower bowl, a process that should take about two minutes. Remove the upper bowl and serve.

Espresso and Cappuccino Machines

It's interesting to realize that today's most exotic coffee maker was actually developed for speed and volume, not necessarily quality. Thus the name espresso. Fortunately, it was developed in Italy, where nothing less than good strong coffee would have been tolerated. Using a gleaming tangle of handles and gauges, the early espresso machines used pressure to channel a mixture of hot water and steam to individual spigots equipped with quickly detachable filters. Big Pavoni machines could turn out 150 cups an hour with this streamlined filtration method, while the expanded La Victoria Arduino produced up to 1,000 cups in that time. The newer, low-slung espresso machines replaced their awkward but beloved ancestors shortly after World War II. With forms better suited to function, these devices sidestep the bitterness caused by occasional overextraction or by scalding the delicate grounds with live steam. Modern espresso machines give steam and water a better chance to mix, making for a smoother-tasting brew. While true espresso should be served in a demitasse, cappuccino is the same strong coffee in a regular six-ounce cup topped with frothy steamed milk. Several of today's espresso machines feature cappuccino attachments as well. Models can cost as much as $700, but the Maxim can be had for $100, the El Espresso

Louis XIV coffee pot with spirit lamp and extinguisher

for $150, the Braun Gaggia for $250 or more and La Pavoni for $450.

A less expensive and less involved alternative to today's wide array of espresso machines is the stovetop device generally known as the Moka-type. This gadget uses heat from a regular burner to produce steam, then uses the steam to force hot water through coffee in a fine vacuum grind. The main caution here is to carefully follow the manufacturer's instructions, especially when dealing with the steam, and to always remove the pot from the heat when all the liquid is gone.

There is also a new line of stovetop espresso makers with such brand names as Bialetti and Morenita that work in much the same manner as manual espresso machines, differing mainly in that they have a rotary valve for water-flow control. While Moka-type coffee makers may start as low as $10 for a three-demitasse-cup capacity, these more complicated stovetops begin around $90 and become more expensive when such accessories as milk-steaming stems and pressure gauges are added. In addition, there is now an exception to the rule that espresso is coffee made under pressure. The Robert Bosch Company of Germany has invented a new system that utilizes no pressure and no enclosed boiler. It is espresso made with centrifugal force and is currently available in the United States for about $100.

Lovers of gadgets are delighted by even the modern, streamlined versions, though their hearts might belong to the more glamorous espresso machines still found in many fine restaurants. Actually, even these turn out to be state-of-the-art, efficient steam engines covered with the gaudy trappings of a century ago. The product they turn out is much better than the old machines could hope to achieve. Home espresso machines are quick and efficient, turning out dark, rich coffee cup by cup, so no reheating or holding is necessary. The devices, for all the extravagance of their past, are much easier to clean than the most proletarian modern percolator. There are, however, some drawbacks, starting with the fact espresso machines are considerably more expensive than other coffee makers. When considering a purchase, insist that the machine can be returned if valves or fittings prove to be leaky, and check for safety valves, warning lights and on-off switches. On some models, the control knobs are too close to hot surfaces for easy handling. Some people may also rebel against the high-pitched scream emitted by the tube spewing milk for cappuccino on some models, but true veterans of the old country consider this the lyrical music of memory.

Technique here is a case of when-in-Rome. Since espresso machines differ wildly, follow the instructions supplied by the manufacturer. If you like a really thick cup of coffee, purchase a Gaggia, Atomic, Vesuviana or Pavoni machine and use two tablespoons of finer-than-vacuum grind coffee to three ounces of water. Moka-type pots, which also use steam to force hot water through the grounds, require a fine vacuum grind. Espresso should be served black with only a twist of lemon peel and sugar, if desired. Cappuccino can be produced with the milk-steaming attachment or nearly duplicated by frothing hot milk in a blender for about a minute and combining it with espresso in equal quantities. This delightful creation can be sweetened with sugar and dusted with cinnamon or nutmeg for a little extra zing (inauthentic though this is).

Pump Percolator

At last, the villain of the piece. On the strength of its convenience, many Americans still make coffee in what by design approaches the worst possible way. The accelerating sound of perking coffee is an essential part of morning to many ears, with the depressing effect of millions of coffee drinkers never having tasted a really fine cup. It is strange that an idea substituting ease for flavor hailed from France originally where quality has almost always come first, though perhaps the Parisian jewelry manufacturer Jacques-Augustin Gandais may be excused for not knowing how his invention would turn out. At least his percolator, which raised boiling water through a tube in the handle, sprayed it over the coffee only once. It was Nicholas Felix Durant who equipped Gandais's design with an inner tube that could pass water through the grounds repeatedly, breaking one of the cardinal rules of good coffee making. Today's electric versions do every bit of damage Durant's once did—only more so. Without your knowing, they can cause underextraction by failing to heat the water enough or overextraction by heating it too much. They can also, of their own or their maker's volition, extend the recommended brewing cycle by up to three times the limit.

The pump percolator's advantages amount to faint praise at best. The cup quality possible is such an affront to good beans that you may as well stick with cheap or even stale ones—an undeniable if indefensible bit of economy. And there are many, many models to choose from, with a wide range of price, size, convenience and brewing speed. Attacking the negatives directly, the coffee tends to be heavy-tasting, oily, nonaromatic and sometimes loaded with sediment, since the production time is longer than for drip models and few percolators are equipped with filters. Many units require that you remove the pump and basket to avoid repercolation, an exercise that often results in burned fingers. Though all such devices require thorough scouring after every use, most are incredibly hard to clean. A special brush is needed to wash out the spout and pump tube.

Heated to boiling, water is forced up through a pump tube to overflow into a basket filled with regular grind coffee. It seeps through and drops back down into the bottom, again and again for up to twenty minutes. At the end of this period, remove the coffee basket and pour out the brew. Electric models feature a thermostat that shuts off the main heating element when the temperature of the coffee nears 200 degrees, and there's a second element on most percolators to keep the brew warm.

The Joys of Grinding Your Own

While many coffee techniques and preferences are simply matters of taste, there is little room for quibbling about the value of grinding your own coffee. Freshness is essential to enjoying the fullest flavor each bean has to offer, and vacuum packing cannot provide the aroma created when you reduce your own favorite beans to your own favorite grind. In addition, grinding coffee ties a satisfying touch of tradition to the brewing process, a bit like growing your own vegetables or bottling your own wine.

The only trick to home grinding is matching the grind to the type of coffee maker used so that all the proportions and times set down by experts are not sabotaged at the start. The finer the grind, the more contact between coffee and water. This speeds up the release of the oils that deliver flavor while cutting down on the release of harsher, less soluble chemicals. Creating a kind of sifted moondust, however, is not a bright idea. Pulverized coffee has no essential oils, as they are destroyed by the heat and friction of the grinding process. A little experimentation goes a long way in this, though it's really fairly easy to find the grind for you.

In all these years, coffee drinkers have come up with only four basic ways of breaking down their beans for brewing. And despite their dizzying variety of styles, grinders currently on the market are only variations on these standard techniques. The oldest way to handle the job is by mortar and pestle, offering the fullest hint possible of what it must have been like in the days of coffee's discovery. After quite a bit of that tedium, frustrated grinders came up with the millstone, which has since been developed into flat steel burrs or corrugated plates. The roller mill was next, but that is used in only the largest commercial operations and therefore holds little interest here. Finally came the electric blade grinder, which applies principles of the ever-popular food blender.

Mortar and Pestle

As you might imagine, there is no cheaper way to grind coffee—and no more intimate involvement either. A mortar and pestle run no more than $10 and can be found for as little as $5. They are also quite lovely to the sympathetic eye, conjuring up visions of magic blacker than even the darkest roast of coffee. The mortar and pestle is not for everybody though, especially considering the time and muscle involved. Yet those who rely on the method insist that it forces a pleasurable contemplation of the bean, its qualities and its relationship to life's larger issues.

Millstone

Early in coffee's history, the people of the Middle East took to doing their grinding with the same sort of heavy apparatus they turned so wearily to make flour from their grain. The Turks scaled the whole business down a good bit, developing a small cylinder with a crank at the top—a forerunner of today's pepper mill. Over time, all sorts of variations appeared, each letting corrugated steel plates do the job once handled by huge millstones. In each of these grinders, whatever their shape, one disk is stationary while the other is rotated by hand or electric motor. The beans are fed in one at a time, ground to a uniform consistency and allowed to fall through the bottom of the grinder. A real advantage of these machines is that the distance between the disks can be adjusted, allowing you to choose and maintain the grind you find most appealing.

Wooden hand-held millstone-type grinders lead the available models in terms of economy. They are made and sold all over the world, with price tags from $8.50 up to around $40. Within that range, the main difference is style, not effectiveness. In all models, beans are fed through a door at the top of the box, pass through the disks, and are deposited, ground, into a drawer at the bottom. The main problem with these grinders is inherent in their design: a tendency to slide around on the table as you turn their too-short handles for the length of time required by their too-small grinding plates. Mounting this design to a table or wall makes all the difference in the world, without making much difference in price.

The large grinders found in grocery stores and specialty shops operate on the same principle as these old-fashioned models. They simply add electricity to replace elbow grease. The push of a button signals the grinder to start working, and it does just that without much assistance until it is stopped. Worthwhile models for the home include the Braun for $62 and the Krups for $65.

Blade Grinders

In this most modern type of grinder, sharp steel blades spin at blinding speed around a cup at the bottom of a receptacle. They don't so much grind as beat the coffee beans to pieces. Unlike the various millstone and burr machines, which let you choose fineness by setting the distance between plates, these gadgets offer only the hope that a longer run will produce a finer grind—and, of course, vice versa. It is no more accurate a system in practice than the theory would lead you to believe.

Electric blade grinders share with the time-worn mortar and pestle a tendency toward unevenness. As any veteran of home grinders will assure you, there always seems to be the finest powder scattered around the blade's far reaches and a batch of frustrating chunks encircling the shaft. With coffee, though, this probably doesn't matter —unless you're going Turkish for the evening and prefer not to have hunks of bean at the bottom of your delicate demitasse. There's also the minor problem of coaxing the coffee out from under the blades. On the bright side, blade grinders are cheap, fast and space efficient. The market breaks down on price almost exclusively, running from the Moulinex at $24.95 to the Braun or Krups at $28.

If you go with any of these models, there are a few hints that will make your life easier. Make certain before buying it that the model's cover fits tightly to keep the fine grounds from flying about and messing up your counter. And no matter what you decide to take home, use a technique known as "pulsing" in the lingo of food processors, since a merciless siege of spinning blades causes far too much heat for the coffee's good. Shoot for spurts of about five seconds while bouncing the grinder just a bit on the counter in hopes of snaring the most elusive remnants of bean.

To Roast or Not to Roast

Coffee lovers who grind their own at home, as well they should, at some point face the inevitable

Dutch East Indies: Roasting coffee in an open pan

temptation to roast their own as well. Certainly, this is a natural step in the ever-deepening appreciation of the bean, not to mention the unavoidable conviction by those who want something done right that they should do it themselves. The trouble is, say the experts, the quality of such roasting is indeed strained, because, unlike grinding, roasting is an art. People spend their entire lives mastering the finer points of Viennese, Full City, Brazilian or Italian, so the job is not one to be taken lightly. Every coffee drinker should own and use a grinder, since the freshness it provides is essential to savoring the varieties of fine coffee from around the world. But roasting is better left to those who do it best, especially with the current convenience of securing a wealth of expert roasts from specialty shops or by mail.

There are, of course, differences of opinion on this—though even those experts who differ say the main reason to roast at home is excitement. They do point out that some people, even today, have trouble obtaining good roasted beans and that a touch of the pioneer spirit may be just the secret to avoiding a future filled with humdrum coffee.

To give home roasting a try is inexpensive and simple enough, since huge commercial roasters are not necessary.

All you need to get started is a lightweight aluminum

pan with a metal handle and a tight-fitting cover, a sturdy oven thermometer that will fit inside the covered pan, store-bought beans roasted the way you like them and a reasonable supply of green coffee.

The beans need only to be kept moving at temperatures of at least 400 degrees and cooled at the correct moment. Hard-surfaced and tough, the best Central and South American beans (Mexicans, Costa Ricans, Guatemalans, Colombians) require a slightly higher temperature to produce pyrolysis—volatilization of the coffee essence. Therefore, they make the best dark roasts.

One simple way of roasting is to place the thermometer in the pan, set the pan on a stovetop flame and cover. Start at a low temperature but keep raising it until the air temperature inside the pan steadies around 500 degrees. Add enough green coffee beans to form a half-inch layer across the bottom and cover again immediately so as not to lose heat. Holding the cover, begin shaking the beans gently and continue to do so at one-minute intervals until the roasting is completed. Make sure with an occasional peek that the thermometer is registering 400 or above.

The start of pyrolysis is announced by the sound of crackling and pungent smoke seeping from under the cover (be sure your kitchen is well ventilated). Shake for a minute or so longer, removing the pan from the flame when the average color of your roasting beans is just a bit lighter than your preroasted sample. Set the cover aside and shake or stir the beans until they are exactly the color of your chosen roast. Don't worry if some are a bit darker than others, since chances are good they will blend together and taste fine when ground and brewed. Dump your batch into a bowl or pan, let them cool and store them in an airtight container just as you would any other coffee.

The Compleat Coffee Lover

Once you have a home grinder and a coffee maker that suit your taste, there is little else you need to enjoy the best in brew for the rest of your life. There is, however, a tantalizing array of convenience and luxury items that can make your life as a coffee lover richer than you ever imagined. They add to coffee drinking the special elegance that it deserves at least occasionally. There are items that assure essential freshness. One special favorite in the Deep South is the Fresh-O-Lator; constructed of heavy gauge aluminum, it holds two pounds of coffee, ground or whole bean, and keeps it at its peak. Costing only $8.50 today, many Fresh-O-Lators are still in use after 30 years in the humid Mississippi River delta. Other choices include contemporary ceramic canisters made by Bee House—nothing more complex than a metal clamp and rubber gasket make an airtight seal. These are priced from $14.50 for the 3½- by 3-inch (7-ounce capacity) variety to $24.50 for the 8 by 5 (45-ounce capacity).

As people learn to demand the best their coffee has to offer, they are less inclined to suffer second-rate brews while on the road. Hence the market for "personal coffee makers." One of the finest available is from Melitta, the only coffee travel kit that features an automatic drip machine. It brews a splendid mug of coffee and travels in a case that holds containers for coffee, cream and sugar, a twelve-ounce ceramic mug, forty filter bags and a scoop. The entire kit is available for $34.50. Also, Corning Design has improved its Coffee on Demand with a new press button for single-handed pouring. This is basically a filter-cone system that keeps the coffee hot for hours in a glass-lined carafe. The sleek servers come in brushed 18/8 stainless steel as well as variously colored enameled aluminum and are priced around $29.50.

Serving is the final stroke, the extra dash that signals and celebrates the end of coffee's long journey. There are several varieties of carafe that dignify any coffee service, depending on the setting and the occasion. For the executive office or boardroom, the classic thirty-two-ounce Alfi confers a sense of prestige. It opens and closes with one hand, and it doesn't spill even if toppled. The Alfi, priced at $95, features a polished chrome surface and a glass liner that keeps coffee hot for a day or longer. Contemporary carafes are also available, great for those who desire something extra without appearing extravagant.

The thirty-three-ounce Corning carafe comes in red, black, sandstone and white, complete with a replaceable glass vacuum liner that does its job for up to twenty hours and a casing of high-impact plastic that resists scuffing, scratching or breaking. It also cleans up with a damp cloth or sponge. This contemporary accessory sells for $29.50.

- A WORD ABOUT ANTIQUES

If your taste runs to antiques when it isn't searching for the perfect bean or roast, coffee paraphernalia offers a fertile field for exploration.

In the late 1800s and early 1900s, the sound of the coffee mill was a typical part of mornings across America. The Sears 1908 catalog offered mills priced from 32 cents to $7.82, the most expensive model favored by stores, hotels and boarding houses for its ability to grind two pounds of coffee per minute. The smaller mills ended up in households, where their price, space-saving size and single-sitting batches were considered important.

With progress, this daily routine became a bit of a novelty, replaced for many by sealed bags or vacuum cans. Some mills were given to children as toys, while others were relegated to storage shelves where they gathered dust and eventually faded from the scene. In the past thirty years, the number of old coffee mills in antique shops, flea markets and auctions has declined significantly.

The main thing to watch for in shopping for old mills is fraud. A large number of modern versions are made to appear antique. Some, of course, are marketed honestly, their old-fashioned touches nothing more than a nice bit of styling. Others, however, have been artificially aged by painting, staining or being left outdoors to weather rapidly. Still others have been gouged, filed, sanded, carved or beaten with tools to take on the trappings of age. Your best protection as a collector is to become knowledgeable and patronize only reputable dealers. A good place to start is a little book by Terry Friend called *Coffee Mills: An Illustrated Price Guide*, published by Collector Books in 1982.

A World of Coffee

- #### THE FRENCH HAVE A WORD FOR IT

You can sit for hours over a single cup, in a Parisian café, reading newspapers brought by your waiter, writing letters or postcards, chatting with friends or simply watching the human parade. Parisian waiters are coldly polite, occasionally welcoming your attempt at French but most often answering in a cruel and correct English. Ordering "café" in the morning summons café au lait, alternately known as *café crème*.

For the well-to-do Parisian, café au lait is accompanied by rolls and butter, sometimes a piece of fruit. The brew is made in a drip pot, then poured into cups simultaneously with scalded milk. For the working person, café au lait is as likely to be served in the traditional white porcelain bowl as a cup; and it often is blended with chicory. With it, a baguette of crisp, fresh bread, to dunk little by little and suck out the liquid as the crust is chewed. Silence is not golden in a laborer's cafe.

Parisian café under the Empire, 1805

In the afternoon, the same order brings café noir or *café nature*, a double dose of dripped coffee poured like liquid ebony into your cup. Café turns up *en demitasse* after the midday and evening meals.

In Flaubert's Normandy a half-and-half mixture of hot black coffee and the local calvados is sweetened with sugar and downed in a delightful absence of ceremony. In the blustery south of France, apples give way to grapes, with *marc* and coffee as the favored restorative. There is also a popular summertime drink known as *mazagran*, a mixture of cold coffee and seltzer water.

- ## LA DOLCE VITA

You can delight in leisurely cups from Rome to Reggio Calabria, but you don't really love Italian coffee unless you love it in train stations. These noisy meeting places, jangling with missed schedules and broadcast proclamations, reveal the true heart of the nation's love affair. And each brew's quality seems enhanced by the fact it is spewed out with a whistle from a web of valves and tubing. In these nervous *stazione*, where speed seems essential except when your train is due, they don't call it espresso for nothing.

Beyond the sounds of whistles and bells, Italian caffès are extraordinary as well. Many of the best can be found along the Corso in Rome, the Toledo in Naples, in the Galleria and Piazza del Duomo in Milan and in the graceful arcades surrounding the Piazza San Marco in Venice. Many of these coffee bars flaunt ornate brass veterans of an earlier era; yet often concealed underneath are the fastest, most efficient espresso machines in the world.

Espresso machines, built as they are both for pragmatism and drama, turn out a glorious array of coffee drinks favored by Italians for generations and now appreciated worldwide. The standard, of course, is espresso itself, a single demitasse of bracing black coffee, drunk with or without sugar and occasionally spiked with a drop of almond or tangerine flavoring. *Espresso Romano* is the same demitasse with a twist or thin slice of lemon on the side, while a *doppio* is a double portion of straight espresso, preferred only by hardy drinkers at the start of a tough day or a long night on the town.

Cappuccino is the second Italian coffee drink to conquer the world at large. Half espresso and half hot frothy steamed milk spewed out into a heavy cup and sweetened, or not, with sugar. *Cafe latte* is similar to café au lait— one or two shots of espresso and three times as much scalded milk in a bowl or cup. *Espresso Machiatto* is a demitasse of espresso "marked" with a tiny quantity of hot, foamed milk, while *latte machiatto* is a huge glass filled with bubbling hot milk and dribbled slowly with a demitasse of espresso. This glass takes on a lovely layered look, pure white foam on top of the dark coffee fading to light at the bottom. Italian *mocha* has nothing to do with the country of Yemen—it's an oversized mug filled with one-third espresso, one-third strong unsweetened hot chocolate and one-third steamed milk. Forty cups of mocha a day was nothing unusual for the great Voltaire, wrapped in thought and sarcasm at the old Café Procope.

• SPAIN

Technically, the coffee in Spanish quick-stop cafés and more elegant sidewalk tables is made along French and Italian lines—dripped through grounds till it is strong, then cut with milk or heavy cream. Despite the similarities, however, the Spanish bring so much emotion to their coffee drinking that it ceases to be a European sidebar and becomes a story all its own.

The natives call their brew *café con leche,* and it will come delightfully thick with milk unless you insist on taking your coffee black. In the cool mornings, dapper executives join stubble-chinned laborers at drop-ins all over Spain, elbowing up to the long brass bars and shouting for their *café.* The beverage, occasionally sweetened before you get it, almost always is served in a small clear glass rather than a cup—its warmth quickly working out to scald your fingers in summer or revive them in the wind-tossed wintertime. In the mountains outside Granada, coffee is often the only heat-producing device that works.

In Andalusia, the favored breakfast on the run is a slice of hard-crusted bread slathered with butter, then browned until crisp. It is so sinfully rich that it goes by the name of butter rather than bread. *"Una mantequilla!"* shout the hurrying workers at the harried men in white behind the bar.

Spain, to those who've never shivered through its winters, is eternally sunny and hot enough for baking outdoors. It is in summer that most visitors stalk its Roman ruins and ornate Moorish monuments, and it is in summer that its matadors return from South America for the only important bullfight season in the world. Andalusians seldom sit down for a proper meal in summer—food simply disappears bit by bit as the day edges forward through shimmering heat. By midafternoon, a Spaniard is likely to spend an hour at a shaded café before heading home for his nap behind closed, dampened shutters. This respite—in Seville, most often along the Calle Sierpes—is a time for gossip, for cigars, perhaps for a glass of sherry. And it's always time for rich, milk-thick cafe, its warmth drawing tiny beads of cooling perspiration to the surface of the skin.

• PORTUGAL

Lisbon is peppered with coffee shops serving samples and coffee houses offering caramel custard as an accompaniment to your brew. In the shops, beans from such former Portuguese possessions as Angola and Mozambique mingle with the best from South America and the Far East. Shopkeepers encourage you to blend your own, even though they sell on site twenty or more single-bean grinds and at least as many standard mixes. Take these entrepreneurs at their word, breathe in the overwhelmingly rich aroma, sip at a sample or three, then have the owner grind several varieties into a bag for you to take away. It's worth making coffee at your hotel just for the experience of buying the beans.

Coffee can serve as warm bookends to a night searching out your favorite *fado*, that Portuguese torch song often compared to the *flamenco* of Spain. First, to the accompaniment of guitars and dark red wine, you grill pieces of *linguiça* or *chouriço* sausage over charcoal at your table.

Then you settle back for the minor-keyed wailing that is the heart of fado, sometimes delivered by paid entertainers and sometimes by shadowy strangers who wander in, toss down a glass of wine, sing a bit of their soul and wander out.

The coffeehouses of Lisbon are lively places indeed, filled to spilling into the streets with men talking sports or business with men, women talking romance or children with women, or men and women blending all those subjects in a way that somehow keeps the race alive. A white-tied waiter delivers your coffee, its blend a secret marriage consummated with nut-bitter hints and mysterious edges of extra flavor. Your *pudim flan* arrives in high style, or your waiter rolls up a glistening cart piled with a wonderland of tiny pastries set on lacy paper doilies. Some are soft and creamy inside, others brittle or flaky. Portuguese coffee, laced with memories of a lost empire, is among the best you'll find anywhere.

• AUSTRIA

In spring and summer, café patrons across Austria flow out onto the streets, sidewalks and public parks, drinking in the pageantry of Vienna or the Mozartian moods of Salzburg. In winter, they disappear behind steamed windows, sipping coffee, reading newspapers and talking politics amid the evolution of today's Europe. There are few places on earth more comfortable than a Viennese café on a rainy winter's afternoon. The coffee is hot, the pastries ambrosial and the conversation contemplative. Men in tweed sit entranced over cup after cup, rising only to trade one periodical for another on the dark wood newspaper rack. Women, though often outnumbered during the day, add their voices to the quiet hum, raising its notes a tiny notch and brightening them around the edges. Nothing intrudes on your enjoyment of one of life's softest single moments.

Coffee here is in the French style, made by the drip method or in a pumping percolator commonly called the Vienna coffee machine. Cafés employ a huge urn fitted with a metal sieve and cloth sack. After ground coffee has infused, a screw device raises the metal sieve and pressure forces the liquid through the cloth sack containing the grounds.

Though world war has twice dimmed their glory, Viennese cafés have struggled up again to a level befitting their pedigree. In the mornings, throngs settle in for coffee and a roll with butter—*mélange* is coffee with milk, *braun* a bit darker than that, *schwarzer* strong and black. In the afternoon and evening it is customary to enjoy your brew with a rich piece of pastry, the famous crescent-shaped Kipfel perhaps, or the sugary jelly square called Krapfel.

Only four Viennese cafés remain in the original locations where the young Secessionists had their *Stammtische* in the golden 1890s. Both the Sperl, founded in 1880, and the Landtmann, dating from the turn of the century, have been refurbished and reupholstered, with copies of the original fabrics woven then and now by Backhausen. The Café Pruckl was redecorated in 1955 but it too has retained its character. The old Café Museum was designed in 1899 by architect Adolf Loos, who rebelled so violently against decoration that he managed to produce a place with no style at all. Even the Charles Dana Gibson room, with all the Gibson girls on the wall, has since been demolished. Yet the café still teems with visitors, many of whom go to spot artists and musicians— and all of whom go for the great coffee.

- SCANDINAVIA

Discouraged by their climate, Swedes, Danes and Norwegians spend less time sipping coffee at sidewalk tables than their counterparts to the south. But they value the beverage all the more, savoring its ever-changing flavors while clinging to its warmth.

Scandinavians reveal a strong French influence when they roast, grind and brew their coffee, though they tend to employ less chicory and more whipped cream. The boiling method also has many followers, especially in the countryside. An open copper kettle is filled with water, coarse-ground coffee is dumped in and boiled. The brew turns out to be delicious, despite a name devoid of lyri-

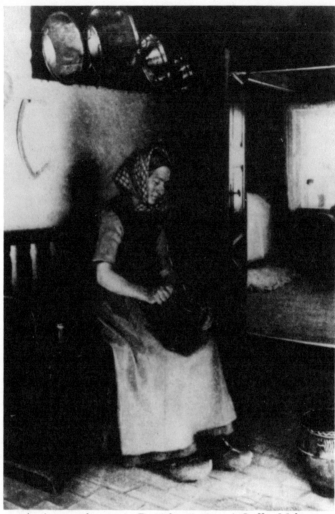

A *nineteenth-century Danish painting*, A Coffee Maker

cism—*grug*. In poorer quarters, cups are filled directly from the kettle, while in more affluent homes silver pots make the transition.

In centuries past, the only real cafés in Norway were the "coffee rooms" of Oslo, tight one-room affairs turning out little more than porridge. Today, however, the gentler customs of the South prevail, with small pockets of tables set out in summer beneath leaves and swaying strings of light.

Everywhere in Norway, you find the cakelike flat bread

lefse, sweeter and less like mashed potatoes than the version turned out by Norwegian-Americans. Norwegians spread their *lefse* with butter, sprinkle it with sugar and cut it into serving pieces, wolfing them down as a quick lunch, as dessert, as accompaniment to coffee day or night. Other memorable coffee companions include sponge cake light enough to float, biscuits stuffed with almonds and currants, heart-shaped waffles and custard tarts called *linser.*

Across Scandinavia, coffee is nothing if not familial. Even in Denmark's finest restaurants, whose chefs serve quail eggs as appetizers and smoke their own salmon and hams, guests retire to the lounge after dinner for double-creamed coffee from a bottomless pot. In Norway, you can see or be seen at Oslo's Gran' Café, though today the crowd is a mix of jeans-clad teenagers and the older, bejeweled and befeathered clientele. Scrambled eggs with smoked salmon are the specialty here, served amid jolly murals and nostalgic piano music from 1900.

Even farther north, at small inns constructed along the edge of fjords, dining is at its most informal, with breakfast a numbing Norwegian buffet and open sandwiches available all day long with a variety of coffee cakes. Whether you've just come in from a stroll along the fjord or finished a simple dinner of fish, it's time for deep-brown, creamy coffee in the inn's dark wooden sitting room.

* GREECE

To walk the quiet quarters of a large Greek city or any street in a small Greek village is to wonder whether any work gets done. Any time of day or night, it seems the entire male population at least is seated at tiny wooden tables, sipping small cups of sludge-like coffee and fondling the ever-present "worry beads."

In Greek homes, spoon sweets are served on dessert plates with ice water—*kafe* either accompanies or follows the sweet. In Athens, people sit for hours over a thick brew around Plateia Syntagmatos, the large Constitution Square facing Parliament. On the smaller Omonia Square or the grounds of the National Archaeological Museum, tables are fewer and groups smaller, yet the slow-moving, appreciative spirit is the same.

The true *kafeneia*, however, exist outside the pull of the modern West and well within the magnetic field of the East. They are for men only, dusty havens from life in the provinces or on any of a hundred sun-washed rock-white islands. The men here play cards, backgammon or billiards. In some of the oldest quarters, the oldest men might smoke a *narghile*, the long-nosed Middle Eastern pipe whose smoke cools as it passes through water.

Some Greek cafes, and especially the less-esteemed outlets known as *zacharoplasteion*, have taken to making their coffee in machines rather than old-fashioned Turkish ibriks. Your palate will quickly assure you that the small, long-handled device is essential—unless you prefer the weak, sediment-free tourist's coffee commonly referred to as "Nescafé." In a coffee shop, you might consider any of the following varieties, each offering a stiff taste of the glory that still is Greece. *Metrios vrastos* is boiled, medium strong, with a minimum of sugar. *Varys glykos* is strong and sweet, while *glykos vrastos* is sweet and boiled. *Sketos* includes no sugar at all.

From Athens to the hinterland, coffee drinkers make much of how their brew is poured—from a height in a steady stream or from the lowest level possible. But if your kafe is prepared properly, with the froth called *kaimake* on top, you will not be disappointed however it is poured.

• TURKEY

In most parts of Turkey today, coffee is not so much served as simply made to appear. There is nary a street so nondescript, from Istanbul to the stark Anatolian plateau, that's not equipped with dark-eyed boys poised to produce the brew at the snap of a finger or the wave of a proper hand. These youths—neatly dressed in the city, urchin-smudgy in the villages—blend with the backdrop until they are needed. Yet they appear instantly when an order is placed, portering the brew on silver trays so spotless they bely the most dilapidated surroundings.

Like nearly all customs in modern Turkey, the cere-

mony attached to coffee has been evolving away from
Oriental extravagance since Ataturk's revolution in 1922.
In tiny pockets of time, however, and tiny pockets of
place, it is still possible to enjoy Turkish coffee with some
of the warmth and consequence it carried in a more be-
nighted but exotic age.

In the Kapali Karsi, the great and glittering bazaar of
Istanbul, a carpet merchant waves you into his stall, sits
you down on a tiny stool and snaps his fingers in the air.
Through a curtain leading to shadowy storage, a boy flows
out bearing demitasses and two clear glasses of water. The
merchant, who resembles Salvador Dali in curling mustache and wild-eyed wonder, sips first at his water, then at
the thick black brew that waits under foam in his cup.
You talk about carpets between your sips, you talk about
price, about life, love, international relations. Then you
rise to leave and the merchant wishes you every happi-
ness. "I am sorry I could find nothing to please you," he
says, smiling under his mustache. "But of course the loser
this time is often the winner the next."

In the countryside, girls and women still wrap scarves
around their faces in a way their grandmothers would

applaud, although Arab-style veils have been outlawed since the revolution. And the men still gather in dens heavy with the wondrous smell of coffee, smoking the bubbling *narghile,* or white meerschaum pipes carved in sultan's heads. A boy delivers coffee and water to the old men sitting along the wall, and so they pass the day.

Recipes:
The Richness of Coffee

Hot and Cold Beverages

ARNAUD'S CAFÉ BRÛLOT

1 orange
16 cloves
Rind of one lemon, grated
4 small cinnamon sticks
4 tablespoons French brandy
4 tablespoons Grand Marnier
4 cups freshly brewed, strong coffee, preferably
  dark roast with chicory
Additional cloves (optional)

To prepare café brûlot for four in the style of Arnaud's in the French Quarter of New Orleans, peel the orange so the rind is a one-piece spiral and stud the rind with cloves if desired. Reserve the fruit of the orange for another use.

Combine the 16 cloves, lemon rind and cinnamon sticks in a flameproof bowl or chafing dish and warm it over a small flame. Then warm a ladle and pour the brandy and Grand Marnier into the ladle.

Attach one end of the orange peel spiral to a long-handled fork. With the lights turned low for effect, ignite the liquid in the ladle and, holding the orange peel over the bowl, pour the flaming liquid down the spiraling orange peel into the bowl. Add 4 cups of freshly brewed coffee to the bowl and stir. Strain the mixture into 4 coffee cups.

Check taste preferences before serving. If a sweeter taste is desired, add a bit of sugar and more Grand Marnier. Serves 4.

THE WINDSOR COURT HOTEL'S CAFE DES DEUX MONDES

Juice of 1 lemon
Sugar
½ cup Galliano liqueur
½ cup Kahlua liqueur
2 cups strong hot coffee, preferably with chicory
½ cup whipped cream, sweetened with 1 tablespoon Amaretto liqueur
Lemon peel shavings (for garnish)

Rub the rims of four wine glasses with lemon juice and dip them in sugar to coat.

One glass at a time, heat the rim of a glass over a small flame. Add the Galliano, ignite it and swirl it over the flame. When the sugar begins to crystallize, add the Kahlua and continue to swirl the glass over the flame until the rim is golden brown and caramelized. Extinguish the flame, add the coffee and whipped cream and garnish with the lemon peel. Repeat the procedure with the other glasses.

Allow the drinks to stand for a minute in order to cool off and allow the whipped cream to filter down into the drink. Drink without a straw. Serves 4.

Café Griensteidl, Vienna, in the nineteenth century

VIENNESE COFFEE

½ teaspoon cinnamon
3 cups hot coffee, French roast
Sweetened whipped cream (for garnish)

Place ⅛ teaspoon cinnamon in each of four dinner cups and fill with coffee. Stir. Top with sweetened whipped cream and serve. Serves 4.

BRANDIED ALMOND COFFEE

2¼ cups hot coffee
4 tablespoons Amaretto liqueur
2 tablespoons brandy
Sweetened whipped cream (for garnish)
Slivered almonds (optional)

Fill four dinner cups two-thirds full with coffee. Add 1 tablespoon Creme de Almond and 1½ teaspoons brandy to each cup. Top with sweetened whipped cream and sprinkle with slivered almonds if desired. Serves 4.

HONEY RUM COFFEE

2 teaspoons honey
2¼ cups hot coffee
4 tablespoons dark rum
1 cup light cream
Nutmeg (for garnish)

Place ½ teaspoon of honey in each of four dinner cups and fill two-thirds full with coffee. Add 1 tablespoon dark rum and ¼ cup light cream to each cup. Sprinkle with nutmeg and serve. Serves 4.

IRISH COFFEE

8 teaspoons sugar
2¼ cups hot coffee, preferably a blend of
*   Mocha and Java*
4 tablespoons Irish whiskey
Sweetened whipped cream (for garnish)

Place 2 teaspoons of sugar into each of four cups and fill three-quarters full with coffee. Add 1 tablespoon of Irish whiskey to each cup and top with sweetened whipped cream. Serves 4.

MEXICAN COFFEE

1 cup light cream
½ cup Kahlua liqueur
2¼ cups hot coffee
Sweetened whipped cream (for garnish)
Cinnamon (for garnish)

Place ¼ cup of light cream and 2 tablespoons of Kahlua into each of four cups, then fill with coffee. Top with sweetened whipped cream and sprinkle with cinnamon. Serves 4.

CAFÉ DON JUAN

1 lemon
Sugar
6 tablespoons rum
½ cup Kahlua liqueur
Hot coffee
2 tablespoons sweetened whipped cream (for
garnish)

Rub the rims of four 8-ounce glasses or goblets with lemon, then dip them in sugar to coat. Hold each of the glasses over a low flame, turning until the sugar melts and adheres to the rim. Pour 1½ tablespoons of rum into each glass and do the following one glass at a time. Ignite the rum, swirling it slowly to keep the liquid flaming for several seconds. Working quickly, add the Kahlua to the flaming rum, all the while swirling the glass, and continue to allow the mixture to flame until the sugar on the rim turns brown. Make sure you swirl the liquid at all times to prevent the hot glass from cracking. Repeat with the other glasses.

Next, pour hot coffee into the glasses to just below the rims of caramelized sugar. Top each with 1½ teaspoons of whipped cream and serve. Serves 4.

COFFEE ROYALE

1 cup whipping cream
2 tablespoons sugar
½ teaspoon cinnamon
½ teaspoon finely grated orange peel
5 cups strong coffee
1¼ cups apricot brandy

In a mixing bowl, combine the whipping cream, sugar, cinnamon and orange peel and whip the mixture until soft peaks form. Chill the whipped cream for several hours until cold.

Combine the coffee and apricot brandy in a saucepan.

Heat through but do not boil. Serve in heatproof glasses or coffee cups. Top each cup with whipped cream mixture. Serves 8.

COFFEE GROG

⅓ cup packed brown sugar
1 tablespoon butter
⅛ teaspoon cinnamon
⅛ teaspoon nutmeg
⅛ teaspoon ground cloves
⅛ teaspoon allspice
4½ cups strong hot coffee
¾ cup rum
¾ cup light cream
6 orange or lemon peel twists (for garnish)

Cream the sugar and butter together in a mixing bowl. Next, blend in the cinnamon, nutmeg, cloves and allspice until completely mixed. Add the coffee, rum and cream and blend well. Then ladle the mixture into six coffee mugs. Garnish each serving with an orange or lemon twist. Serve immediately. Serves 6.

GINGERED WHISKEY COFFEE

2 tablespoons peeled and chopped fresh ginger
    root
¾ cup whiskey
2½ cups freshly brewed hot coffee
⅓ cup heavy cream, whipped (for garnish)

In a small bowl, soak the ginger in the whiskey overnight. Strain out the ginger, reserving the whiskey. Divide the whiskey evenly among four coffee cups. Fill the cups with coffee and top with a dollop of whipped cream. Serves 4.

Louis XIV
silver coffee pot

FRENCH COFFEE WITH PERNOD

4 cups strong coffee
2 tablespoons sweetened chocolate syrup
2½ tablespoons sugar
12 whole cloves
2 cinnamon sticks
½ teaspoon Pernod, or more to taste
8 strips lemon zest (for garnish)
8 strips orange zest (for garnish)
¼ cup heavy cream, whipped (for garnish)

In a deep chafing dish or medium saucepan, combine the coffee, chocolate syrup, sugar, cloves, cinnamon sticks and Pernod. Steep the mixture over very low heat for 15 minutes to infuse the flavors. Spoon out the cinnamon sticks and cloves. Then ladle the hot coffee into small mugs or demitasse cups. Add a strip of lemon or orange zest to each cup and top with a spoonful of the whipped cream. Serves 16.

CAFÉ ARUBA

3 cups strong coffee
¼ cup orange peel cut in thin slices, with all
white pith removed

> 1 orange, peeled and sliced
> 1 tablespoon sugar
> 1 teaspoon aromatic bitters
> ½ cup whipping cream, whipped and
>   sweetened to taste (for garnish)

Measure hot coffee into a flameproof glass pot, then add the orange peel and slices. Steep over low heat for about 15 minutes. Add sugar and bitters. Do not boil. Strain and pour into warmed heatproof glasses. Top with whipped cream. Serves 4 or 5.

BELGIAN COFFEE

> 1 egg white
> ¼ teaspoon vanilla extract
> ½ cup whipping cream
> 4 cups hot coffee
> Chocolate curls (for garnish)
> Sugar (optional)

Beat the egg white until stiff peaks form. In a separate bowl, add the vanilla to the whipping cream and beat until it forms peaks. Fold the egg white into the cream.

Fill four heatproof glasses one-third full with the

*A silver coffee pot
from Bruges, 1772*

whipped cream mixture, then top them off with the hot coffee. The whipped mixture will float to the top. Garnish with chocolate curls and serve at once, with sugar if desired. Serves 4.

OLD DUTCH COFFEE

2 cups strong hot coffee
2 tablespoons crème de cacao liqueur
2 tablespoons chocolate mint liqueur
Whipped cream (for garnish)
Chocolate flakes or grated chocolate (for
garnish)

Combine coffee with liqueurs and serve in heatproof glass mugs. Garnish with whipped cream and chocolate flakes or grated chocolate. Serves 3 or 4.

FLAMING BRANDIED COFFEE

4 teaspoons sugar
2¼ cups hot coffee
4 tablespoons brandy

Place 1 teaspoon of sugar in each demitasse cup and fill it three-quarters full with hot coffee. Carefully float 1 tablespoon brandy on top of each cup. Ignite the brandy in each cup, then stir and serve. Serves 4.

ORANGE COFFEE

½ cup curaçao liqueur
2¼ cups hot coffee
8 orange peel twists (for garnish)

Place 1 tablespoon of curaçao into each of eight demitasse cups and fill with coffee. Serve with twists of orange peel. Serves 8.

COFFEE MILANO

½ cup ground coffee
¼ teaspoon cinnamon
1 slightly beaten egg white
Sugar
6 tablespoons Galliano liqueur
¼ cup coffee liqueur, such as Kahlua
Whipped cream (for garnish)

Place the ground coffee in the basket of your coffee maker, then sprinkle the cinnamon over the top. Using 4 cups of water, prepare the coffee according to manufacturer's instructions. Next dip the rims of six small brandy snifters in the slightly beaten egg white, then in sugar. Place 1 tablespoon Galliano liqueur and ⅔ teaspoon coffee liqueur into each snifter. Pour in ⅔ cup coffee and top with whipped cream. Serves 6.

ITALIAN COFFEE

4 cups hot coffee
4 tablespoons Strega liqueur
Lemon peel twists (for garnish)
Sugar

Add Strega to coffee and pour into demitasse cups. Serve with lemon peel twists and sugar. Serves 8.

CHANTILLY

2¼ cups hot coffee
4 tablespoons cognac
Heavy cream

Fill dinner cups two-thirds full with coffee, then add 1 tablespoon of cognac to each cup. Float cream on top and serve. Serves 4.

*Russian coffee pot,
1898*

Café Russe

4 tablespoons Kahlua
4 tablespoons vodka
2 cups strong hot coffee
Whipped cream (for garnish)

For each serving, blend together 1 tablespoon Kahlua and 1 tablespoon vodka in a heatproof glass or coffee cup. Add ½ cup coffee to each and stir. Top each serving with whipped cream. Serves 4.

Hisae's Kioki Coffee

2 cups hot coffee
4 tablespoons Kahlua liqueur
2 tablespoons brandy
Whipped cream (for garnish)

Stir together the coffee, Kahlua and brandy in a heat-proof pitcher or other container. Divide the mixture evenly among four wine glasses. Top each glass with whipped cream. Serves 4.

Chocolate Chip Coffee

4 tablespoons Kahlua liqueur
2 tablespoons crème de menthe liqueur
2 cups hot coffee
Whipped cream (for garnish)
4 tablespoons chocolate liqueur (for garnish)

Add the Kahlua and crème de menthe to the coffee in a heatproof pitcher or other container. Divide the mixture evenly into four large wine glasses. Top each with whipped cream, then sprinkle with the chocolate liqueur to resemble chocolate chips. Serves 4.

James Farr at the Rainbow in Fleet Street, his halfpenny token

Cold Drinks

Caffè Diavolo

2 tablespoons unflavored gelatin
4 tablespoons instant coffee
1 stick cinnamon
3 whole cloves
½ cup sugar
3 tablespoons rum
2 tablespoons Amaretto di Saronno liqueur
Whipped cream (for garnish)

Soften the gelatin in ½ cup of cold water and set aside. In a small saucepan, combine 2¾ cups cold water with the next four ingredients, bring to a boil and simmer for 5 minutes. Remove spices. Add gelatin and stir until dissolved. Stir in rum and Amaretto.

Pour into eight individual serving glasses. Chill until firm and serve with a puff of whipped cream on top. Serves 8.

SPICED ICED COFFEE

8 cups coffee
1 whole cinnamon stick
8 whole cloves
Cream
Sugar to taste

When the coffee is brewed, add the cinnamon stick and cloves. Allow the mixture to cool, then refrigerate it until chilled. Put some ice cubes in tall glasses and strain the coffee over the ice. Pour cream into the coffee just before serving. Serve with sugar. Serves 6.

MRS. SAURAGE'S COFFEE COOLER

1 quart good-quality vanilla ice cream
4 cups strong hot coffee
Whipped cream (for garnish)

Place a scoop of ice cream in each of six tall glasses. Pour hot coffee carefully over the ice cream until each glass is about two-thirds full, then add a second scoop of ice cream and more coffee. Garnish with whipped cream. Serves 6.

COFFEE EGGNOG

6 eggs, separated
2 cups half-and-half
2 cups whole milk
¾ cup sugar
1 cup brandy
2 cups light rum
3 cups strong cooled coffee
Dash of salt
1 cup heavy cream
Nutmeg (for garnish)

Beat the egg yolks until thick and lemon colored. Blend in the half-and-half, milk, sugar, brandy, rum, coffee and the dash of salt. Beat the egg whites until stiff but not dry. In another bowl, whip the cream. Then fold the egg whites into the yolk mixture and fold the whipped cream into the eggnog. Pour the eggnog into a punch bowl and sprinkle it with nutmeg. Serves 24.

BROWN GRASSHOPPER

2¼ cups fresh cold coffee
4 tablespoons brandy
2 tablespoons white crème de menthe
1½ pints good-quality vanilla ice cream

Place cold coffee and remaining ingredients into a blender. Blend until frothy. Serves 8.

FROSTY CAFÉ AU LAIT

2¼ cups cold coffee
2 cups milk
2 cups crushed ice
Sugar (optional)

Place all ingredients in a blender. Add sugar if desired and blend until frothy. Serve over ice. Serves 8.

CHOCOLATE MINT COOLER

2¼ cups cold coffee
4 tablespoons crème de cacao
4 tablespoons white crème de menthe
1 cup light cream
Ice cubes of frozen coffee or regular ice cubes

Place the cooled coffee, liqueurs and light cream into a blender. Blend until frothy. Serve over ice cubes, preferably those made by freezing coffee in an ice cube tray. Serves 4.

COCONUT CLOUDS

2 cups whole milk
2 tablespoons sugar
1 3½-ounce can (1⅓ cups) flaked coconut
2 cups strong hot coffee
Whipped cream (for garnish)
Toasted coconut (for garnish)

Combine the milk, sugar and flaked coconut in a saucepan. Heat and stir it over a low flame until mixture steams, then pour into blender. Cover and blend until smooth. Strain.

In the same saucepan, combine the milk mixture and coffee. Heat through but do not boil. Pour into four heat-proof glasses or coffee cups. Top each serving with a dollop of whipped cream and a pinch of toasted coconut. Serves 4.

MOCHA MILK PUNCH

1 quart good-quality coffee ice cream
1 cup strong chilled coffee
1 cup whole milk
¼ cup bourbon
¼ cup light rum
¼ cup crème de cacao

Combine half the ice cream in a blender with the coffee, milk, bourbon, rum and crème de cacao. Cover and blend until smooth. Pour into six glasses. Top each serving with a scoop of the remaining ice cream. Serves 6.

Sagafjord Coffee Mexico

2 cups soft good-quality coffee ice cream
½ cup plus 2 tablespoons fresh pineapple
    cubes
½ cup fresh banana slices
1 cup tequila
½ cup whipped cream (for garnish)

Spoon the soft coffee ice cream into 4 large glasses. Combine the pineapple cubes, banana slices and tequila and pour the mixture on top of the ice cream in each glass. Garnish each serving with whipped cream. Serves 4.

Rum Runner

2¼ cups cold coffee
1 cup dark rum
1 quart good-quality vanilla ice cream

Place the cold coffee and remaining ingredients into a blender and blend until smooth. Serve in cocktail glasses. Serves 8.

Coffee Banana Shake

1 cup chilled coffee
2 medium-ripe bananas, sliced
1 pint good-quality coffee ice cream
2 tablespoons sugar
1 or 2 drops almond flavoring

Pour the coffee into a blender, then add the bananas, ice cream, sugar and almond flavoring. Cover and blend at high speed until thick and fluffy. Pour into chilled glasses. Serves 3 or 4.

STRAWBERRY BREEZE

1 cup chilled coffee
1 cup light cream
3 tablespoons sugar
1 cup strawberries
½ cup crushed ice

Combine the coffee in a blender with the light cream, sugar, strawberries and crushed ice. Cover and blend at high speed until foamy. Pour into chilled tall glasses. Serves 2 or 3.

DANISH COGNACKAFFEE

6 eggs, chilled
Grated peel of 1 lemon
½ cup sugar
3 cups strong cold coffee
⅔ cup brandy or cognac

Beat the eggs and lemon peel until light and fluffy. Add the sugar gradually while continuing to beat the mixture until it is thick. Stir the coffee in slowly, then add the cognac or brandy. Divide the mixture evenly into twelve chilled 4-ounce glasses. Serves 12.

ICED COFFEE NEW YORK

¾ cup good-quality strawberry ice cream
2 cups cold coffee
1 cup bourbon
8 tablespoons whipped cream (for garnish)
4 tablespoons grated chocolate (for garnish)

Spoon the strawberry ice cream into four serving glasses. Evenly divide the coffee and bourbon and add them to the glass. Stir. Garnish each serving with 2 table-spoons whipped cream and 1 tablespoon chocolate. Serves 4.

ICED COFFEE STRASBOURG

¾ cup good-quality banana ice cream
2 cups cold coffee
1 cup Grand Marnier
½ cup whipped cream (for garnish)
4 tablespoons toasted almonds (for garnish)

Spoon the ice cream evenly into four serving glasses. Then add an equal amount of coffee and Grand Marnier to each glass. Garnish each with whipped cream and toasted almonds. Serves 4.

An English coffee-house scene

Entrées, Side Dishes and Breads

BEEF À BRASILEIRA

¼ cup (4 tablespoons) butter
2 pounds cubed beef (round steak or stewing
beef)
1 clove garlic, crushed
3 onions, sliced
¼ cup wheat flour
¾ cup dry white wine
2 teaspoons salt
½ teaspoon oregano
1 cup strong coffee
6 portions of cooked rice

Melt the butter and brown the meat in a deep skillet. Then sauté the garlic and onions with the meat. Remove the meat and onions from the skillet with a slotted spoon.

In the same skillet, mix the flour with the remaining butter, then add the wine, salt, oregano and coffee. Cook the mixture, stirring until slightly thickened, then return the meat and onions to skillet. Cover and bring to a boil. Lower the heat and simmer the mixture for 1½ hours or until the meat is tender. Serve over rice. Serves 6.

BOSTON BAKED BEANS

1 medium onion
½ teaspoon dry mustard
Salt and pepper
2 1-pound cans Boston-style baked beans
½ cup molasses
½ cup strong coffee
¼ pound fat salt pork

Peel the onion and place in a bean pot or deep casserole dish. Then mix in the dry mustard along with salt and pepper to taste. Pour in the baked beans and mix well.

Combine the molasses, coffee and ½ cup boiling water in a separate heatproof container and pour over the beans. Scrape the pork rind and score it with a sharp knife. Bury the pork in the beans, leaving the rind exposed. Bake the casserole in a 350-degree oven for 1 hour. Serves 6 to 8.

SPECIAL CHILI

1 medium onion, minced
1 pound ground beef
1 tablespoon vegetable oil
1 tablespoon chili powder
¼ teaspoon cayenne pepper
½ cup coffee
1 small can green chilis
2 cups kidney beans, canned
2 cups beef broth
1 cup shredded Cheddar cheese (optional)

Sauté the onion with the ground beef in the oil. Then stir in the chili powder, cayenne, coffee, chilis, beans, broth and 2 cups of water. Bring the mixture to a boil. stirring constantly. Then lower the heat and simmer it for 20 minutes. Serve in bowls topped with shredded Cheddar cheese, if desired. Serves 4.

SHISH KEBAB

½ cup chopped onion
½ cup strong coffee
2 tablespoons lemon juice
2 tablespoons olive oil
1 teaspoon salt
¼ teaspoon dried thyme, crushed
⅛ teaspoon pepper
1½ pounds boneless lamb, cut into 1-inch
    pieces
12 large fresh mushrooms

2 medium green peppers, cut into 1½-inch
pieces
12 cherry tomatoes

For the shish kebab marinade, combine the onion in a bowl with the coffee, lemon juice, olive oil, salt, thyme and pepper. Add the meat, cover and refrigerate several hours, overnight if possible.

Drain the meat, reserving the marinade. Set both aside. Pour some boiling water over the mushrooms, let them stand for 1 to 2 minutes and drain.

Thread the meat pieces on skewers, alternating with the green pepper pieces and mushrooms. Grill the kebabs over hot coals for 10 to 12 minutes, brushing them with the marinade and turning them often. Add the cherry tomatoes to the skewers and grill the kebabs for 1 to 2 minutes more. Serves 6.

An Arab coffee house in Cairo

STUFFED PEPPERS

6 large green peppers
¼ cup (4 tablespoons) butter
1 large red onion, peeled and minced
½ pound lean ground pork
½ pound lean ground beef
½ teaspoon salt
½ teaspoon pepper
½ cup seedless raisins
2 cups cooked rice
1 cup coffee
1 egg, well beaten
¼ cup pignoli nuts (optional)
3 tablespoons dry breadcrumbs

Boil the whole peppers in a large saucepan for 2 to 3 minutes, using just enough water to cover them. Then drain them and dry them carefully to remove any wax. Cut off the stem ends, then scoop out the white membrane and seeds.

Melt the butter in a large skillet, add the onion and sauté until it is limp. Then add the pork and beef and cook the mixture until lightly browned before adding all the remaining ingredients except the breadcrumbs. Cook the mixture over medium heat for 6 to 8 minutes, until it is blended or until the liquid is absorbed.

Preheat the oven to 350 degrees. Stuff the peppers with the meat mixture and sprinkle them lightly with the breadcrumbs. Place the peppers in a baking pan, add a little water and cover with aluminum foil. Bake for 15 minutes, then remove the foil and bake for another 15 to 20 minutes. Serves 6.

TRADITIONAL SOUTHERN HAM WITH RED-EYE GRAVY

3 slices country ham, sliced ⅛ inch thick
Lard, ham fat or cooking oil
½ cup strong coffee

Cut the ham slices in half and trim off the fat, reserving the trimmings. Cook the trimmings in a skillet until crisp and about 2 tablespoons of drippings accumulate, then discard the trimmings. Some cooking oil or lard should be added if necessary to produce 2 tablespoons in the skillet.

Cook the ham in the skillet in the hot drippings until it is browned on both sides and the fat is translucent, about 5 minutes on each side. Remove the ham to a warm platter and keep it warm.

Heat the skillet until it is very hot. Add the coffee quickly, taking care to avoid splattering. Cook, scraping the pan to remove the crusty bits, until the mixture boils vigorously. Continue cooking over high heat for 3 minutes, or until the mixture is reduced by half.

Pour the mixture into a bowl. The gravy will form two layers. Serve hot over the ham slices. Serves 4.

BARBECUED SPARERIBS

5–6 pounds spareribs, cut into serving-size
    pieces
1 cup strong coffee
½ cup molasses
¼ cup prepared mustard
1 tablespoon Worcestershire sauce
½ cup cider vinegar
Tabasco sauce (to taste)

Preheat the oven to 350 degrees.

Arrange the spareribs in a single layer in a large, shallow roasting pan. Combine the remaining ingredients in a saucepan over low heat and heat and stir until blended. Brush the mixture lavishly over the ribs.

Place in the oven and bake uncovered for 2½ hours, basting frequently with the remaining sauce.

Spareribs may also be barbecued over a charcoal fire and basted with this sauce, if preferred.

Serves 8.

Sauce for Roast Pork

⅔ cup strong coffee
⅓ cup (5 tablespoons plus 1 teaspoon)
    unsalted butter
2 teaspoons Worcestershire sauce
1½ teaspoons dry mustard
1 tablespoon lemon juice
1 teaspoon sugar
Tabasco sauce (to taste)

Combine all the ingredients in a saucepan. Heat gently, stirring until the butter melts. Then brush over pork during roasting. Serve what is left in a sauceboat. Makes 1½ cups.

Café Glazed Ham

1 5- to 6-pound tenderized ham
1 cup honey
¾ cup strong coffee
½ teaspoon cinnamon
½ teaspoon ground ginger
½ teaspoon allspice

Score the fat on the ham, then bake 30 minutes for each pound at 325 degrees.

An hour before the ham is finished, combine the remaining ingredients for the glaze in a saucepan and simmer for 10 to 15 minutes. Baste the ham with the café glaze during the final 45 minutes of baking. Serves 8.

Meatballs Piemonte

2 pounds lean ground beef
1½ cloves garlic, crushed
1 medium onion, finely chopped
¼ teaspoon savory

¼ teaspoon oregano
¼ teaspoon paprika
2 teaspoons salt
1 cup breadcrumbs
1 tablespoon prepared mustard
1 dash Tabasco sauce
2 teaspoons Worcestershire sauce
Flour
4 strips raw bacon, cut into small pieces
1 cup strong coffee
½ cup red wine, preferably Burgundy
1 teaspoon salt
1 teaspoon sugar
1½ tablespoons flour
1 cup sour cream

In a bowl, combine the ground beef, garlic, onion, herbs, salt, breadcrumbs, mustard, Tabasco and Worcestershire and mix well. Form the mixture into approximately 30 meatballs and dust them with flour.

Cook the bacon until crisp and brown and remove it from the pan. Sauté the meatballs in the bacon drippings until lightly browned. Add the coffee, wine, ½ cup of water, salt and sugar and simmer 15 minutes.

Return the bacon to the pan. Make a smooth paste with the flour and ¼ cup of cold water and stir it into the pan. Cook the mixture gently for 5 more minutes and reduce the heat. Garnish each serving with dollops of sour cream. Serves 6 to 8.

Leather token from
the Union Coffee House
in Cornhill

BETTER-THAN-MAMA'S MEATLOAF

1½ pounds lean ground beef
1 pound lean ground veal
½ pound lean ground pork
1½ cups soft breadcrumbs

¾ cup plus 2 tablespoons cold coffee
1 egg, slightly beaten
1 tablespoon prepared mustard
1 tablespoon Worcestershire sauce
1 teaspoon salt
6 medium white potatoes
¼ cup (4 tablespoons) butter
¼ cup minced onion
2 10-ounce packages frozen mixed vegetables,
    partly thawed
1 tablespoon minced parsley

Preheat the oven to 350 degrees. Lightly oil a 10-inch ring mold. Combine the beef, veal, pork, breadcrumbs, ¾ cup of the coffee, the egg, mustard, Worcestershire sauce and salt and blend them well. Pack the mixture into the mold lightly and bake it for 45 to 50 minutes.

The originator of this recipe traditionally serves the ring of meatloaf with a garnish of mashed potatoes and frozen vegetables nestled in the center hole. It can also be served more simply with any vegetable on the side.

If you wish to make the mashed potatoes and vegetable garnish, boil the potatoes in enough water to cover them until they are tender. Peel them while they are still hot and mash them with 3 tablespoons of the butter until they are smooth. Set aside and keep them warm.

In a medium saucepan, sauté the onion in the remaining tablespoon of butter until it is limp, then add the frozen vegetables, 4 tablespoons of water and the remaining 2 tablespoons of coffee. Bring the mixture to a boil and cover it. Lower the heat.

Cook the vegetables until they are tender, then drain them and add the hot cooking liquid to the mashed potatoes. Beat the potatoes until they are blended. Then fold the cooked vegetables and the minced parsley into the mashed potatoes.

To serve, unmold the meatloaf on a warm serving platter and fill the center of the ring with mashed potatoes and vegetables. Pass the remaining vegetables separately. Serves 6 to 8.

BREAKFAST HASH

3 *tablespoons butter*
1 *onion, chopped*
1 *green pepper, chopped*
2 *1-pound cans corned beef hash*
½ *cup coffee*
2 *teaspoons Worcestershire sauce*
2 *teaspoons Dijon mustard*
6 *tablespoons sour cream*
Salt and pepper
¼ *cup minced parsley*

Melt the butter in a skillet, then sauté the onion and green pepper over medium heat until soft. Add the corned beef hash and break it up. Add the coffee and simmer until it is absorbed.

Add the Worcestershire sauce, mustard, sour cream and seasonings to taste. Simmer for 3 minutes, being careful not to let the mixture boil. Sprinkle with the parsley and serve with some eggs and fresh biscuits. Serves 6 to 8.

BEEF BRETONNE

¼ *cup (4 tablespoons) butter*
3 *pounds round steak, cut into ¾-inch cubes*
1 *clove garlic, crushed*
3 *onions, sliced*
4 *tablespoons flour*
½ *cup red wine, preferably Burgundy*
2 *teaspoons salt*
½ *teaspoon pepper*
¼ *teaspoon rosemary*
¼ *teaspoon oregano*
1 *cup strong cold coffee*

In a deep frying pan, melt the butter and brown the cubed steak on all sides. Add the garlic and onions, cooking until the onions are soft but not brown. Remove the meat and onions from the pan.

Blend the flour with the butter remaining in the pan. Then add the wine, ½ cup of water, seasonings and coffee. Stir the mixture over low heat until it is slightly thickened. Return the meat and onions to the pan, cover and bring to a boil. Reduce the heat and simmer for 1½ hours, or until the meat is tender. Serves 6.

COFFEE-CREAMED
CARROTS AND POTATOES

2 cups thinly sliced carrots
½ teaspoon salt
6 small new potatoes, unpeeled and boiled
1 cup sour cream, at room temperature
½ cup cold coffee
1 teaspoon paprika

With just enough water to cover the carrots, boil them with the salt in a large saucepan until they are tender and almost dry. Drain the carrots and keep them hot.

Cut the boiled potatoes into quarters and add them to the carrots. In another bowl, mix the sour cream and coffee together, then add the mixture to the vegetables and heat it until it is steaming, being careful not to let it boil.

Transfer the mixture to a serving dish and sprinkle the top with paprika. Serve at once. Serves 6.

ORANGES STUFFED WITH
SWEET POTATOES
AND COFFEED RAISINS

½ cup raisins
½ cup coffee
1 29-ounce can sweet potatoes, mashed
2 teaspoons baking powder
¼ cup (4 tablespoons) butter

½ cup brown sugar
Grated peel of half a small orange
½ cup chopped walnuts
1 teaspoon cinnamon
1 tablespoon sugar
5 small oranges

Preheat the oven to 350 degrees.

Mix the raisins and coffee. Heat through (preferably for 30 seconds in a microwave) and let the mixture stand until the raisins get plump. Then add all the other ingredients except the oranges.

Cut the oranges in half, preferably with a decorative edge, scoop them out and fill them with the mixture. Heat the stuffed oranges until they are warm, about 20 minutes. Serves 10.

HEIDELBERG RYE

3 to 3½ cups all-purpose flour
¼ cup unsweetened cocoa powder
2 packages (1 tablespoon plus 1 teaspoon)
    active dry yeast
1 tablespoon caraway seeds
2 cups strong hot coffee
⅓ cup light molasses
2 tablespoons butter
1 tablespoon sugar
1 tablespoon salt
3 cups rye flour
Cooking oil

Combine 2½ cups of the all-purpose flour, the cocoa powder, yeast and caraway seeds in a large mixing bowl. In another bowl, combine the hot coffee, molasses, butter, sugar and salt. Stir the mixture until the butter melts. Cool the coffee mixture to 115 degrees, then add it to the flour mixture.

Beat the ingredients at low speed with an electric mixer for 30 seconds, scraping the bowl frequently. Beat the mixture another 3 minutes at high speed. Stir in the rye flour and as much of the remaining all-purpose flour as you can mix in with a spoon.

Turn the dough out onto a lightly floured surface. In a total of 6 to 8 minutes, knead in enough of the remaining flour to make the dough moderately stiff. Shape it into a ball, cover it and let it rest for 20 minutes. Then punch the ball down and divide it in half, shaping each half into a round loaf.

Place the loaves on greased cookie sheets or in two greased 9-inch pie plates. Flatten the loaves to 6 inches in diameter, then brush the surface of the loaves with a little cooking oil. Slash the tops with a sharp knife.

Let the dough rise until it doubles, 45 to 60 minutes, then bake it in a preheated oven at 375 degrees for 25 to 30 minutes or until done.

Remove the loaves from the cookie sheets or pans and brush them again with a bit of cooking oil to produce a shinier surface. Cool the loaves on wire racks. Makes 2 loaves.

Newspaper hog in a Vienna coffee house

SICILIAN BREAD

2 tablespoons vegetable shortening
1 tablespoon butter at room temperature
1 cup coffee
1 tablespoon molasses
2 teaspoons salt
2 envelopes (1 tablespoon plus 1 teaspoon)
    active dry yeast
1 tablespoon sugar
4 cups all-purpose flour
1¾ cups cracked wheat
¼ cup cornmeal
2 teaspoons whole milk

Combine the shortening, butter, coffee, molasses and salt in a small saucepan. Stir over low heat until the mixture is smooth. Cool it to lukewarm.

Put the yeast and sugar in a large bowl, then add 1 cup of warm water. Let it stand for about 10 minutes, until the yeast dissolves and the mixture is bubbly. Add the coffee mixture and 2 cups of the flour. Beat the ingredients at low speed with an electric mixer for 30 seconds. Stir in the cracked wheat with a wooden spoon until it is blended, then stir in the remaining 2 cups of flour. Cover the dough and let it rise in a warm place until it has doubled in bulk.

Knead the dough on a lightly floured surface for 1 minute. Divide it in half and shape each half into a ball. Cover the dough and let it rise in a warm place until it has doubled in bulk once more.

Sprinkle a cookie sheet evenly with the cornmeal and set it aside. On a lightly floured surface, knead each ball of dough for about 1 minute, then shape them into two long, narrow loaves. Place them on the cookie sheet. With a sharp knife, make 3 or 4 diagonal cuts about ¼ inch deep across the tops of the loaves. Cover them and again let them rise until they have doubled in bulk.

Preheat the oven to 375 degrees. Place a shallow pan of water on the bottom rack to create steam to help the crusts harden. Brush the tops of the loaves with the milk to help them brown and bake them for 35 to 40 minutes.

If they brown too quickly, cover them loosely with aluminum foil. Makes 2 loaves.

FINNISH BRAIDS

6 to 6⅓ cups all-purpose flour
2 packages (1 tablespoon plus 1 teaspoon)
   active dry yeast
½ teaspoon ground cardamom
1 cup strong hot coffee
½ cup (1 stick) butter
½ cup sugar
1 teaspoon salt
2 eggs
1 tablespoon finely shredded orange peel
⅓ cup orange juice
1 egg yolk
1 tablespoon whole milk or water

Combine 2 cups of the flour, the yeast and the ground cardamom in a large mixing bowl.

In a separate bowl, combine the hot coffee, butter, sugar and salt. Stir until the butter melts, then cool to 115 degrees before adding the coffee mixture to the flour mixture.

Add the eggs, orange peel and juice. Beat the ingredients at low speed with an electric mixer for 30 seconds, scraping the bowl frequently. Then beat 3 minutes at high speed.

Stir in as much of the remaining flour as you can with a spoon, then turn the dough out onto a lightly floured surface. Knead in enough of the leftover flour to make a moderately soft dough, kneading for a total of 5 to 8 minutes. Then shape the dough into a ball, place it in a lightly greased bowl and turn once so that the dough is greased on both sides. Cover and let it rise in a warm place until the dough doubles in bulk, about 1 hour.

Punch down the dough and divide it in half, then divide each half into thirds for a total of six pieces. Shape each piece into a ball, cover them and let them rest for 10 minutes.

Roll each ball into a 16-inch-long rope. Line up three of the ropes, an inch apart, on a greased cookie sheet. Braid them loosely, beginning in the middle and working toward the ends. Shape the braid into a ring, pinching the ends together and tucking them under. Repeat this procedure with the remaining three ropes.

Cover the rings and let them rise in a warm place until they have almost doubled in bulk, about 30 minutes.

Preheat the oven to 350 degrees. Lightly beat the egg yolk and milk or water together. Right before baking, brush the braids with the egg mixture. Bake the braids for 25 to 30 minutes, or until they are golden. Cover them loosely with foil for the final 5 to 10 minutes to prevent them from overbrowning. Makes 2 loaves.

SPECIAL SOUTHERN CORNBREAD

1 teaspoon vinegar
¾ cup milk, at room temperature
4 slices raw bacon
1 cup yellow cornmeal
1 cup all-purpose flour
1 teaspoon baking powder
½ teaspoon baking soda
¾ cup coffee, at room temperature
1 egg

Stir the vinegar into the milk and set it aside.

Cook the bacon over low heat in a heavy 9- to 10-inch skillet until all the fat is rendered and the slices are crisp. Reserve the drippings. Drain the bacon on some paper towels and crumble it. Set it aside.

Preheat the oven to 450 degrees. Pour all but a thin film of the bacon drippings into a measuring cup. Discard all but ¼ cup of the drippings and set aside. Place the skillet over low heat. In a medium bowl, combine the cornmeal, flour, baking powder and baking soda. Make a well in the center and pour the milk-vinegar mixture into it.

Add the coffee and the egg, blending the mixture with a fork. Add the reserved drippings and crumbled bacon. Blend the mixture well but quickly. Pour the cornbread back into the heated skillet. Then bake it in the preheated oven for 20 to 25 minutes, until the cornbread is firm and lightly browned on top. Cut it into wedges. Serves 6 to 8.

Desserts and Other Delights

COFFEE PUMPKIN CHIFFON PIE

3 eggs, separated
⅔ cup sugar
1½ cups canned pumpkin (unseasoned)
⅓ cup strong coffee
½ teaspoon salt
½ teaspoon powdered ginger
½ teaspoon cinnamon
½ teaspoon nutmeg
1 envelope unflavored gelatin
¼ cup strong cold coffee
1 cup whipping cream
1 9-inch baked pie crust (recipe follows)

Beat the egg yolks. Add ⅓ cup of the sugar, the pumpkin, the ⅓ cup of coffee, the salt and the spices. Transfer the mixture to the top of a double boiler and stir it over hot, not boiling, water until it is hot.

Sprinkle the gelatin on the remaining ¼ cup of coffee. Dissolve this in the hot pumpkin mixture and chill it for 30 minutes, until it is slightly thickened.

Beat the egg whites until they are stiff and add the remaining ⅓ cup of sugar while continuing to beat. Fold the egg whites into the pumpkin mixture. Whip ½ cup of the cream and fold it in. Then spoon the filling into the baked pie crust (see recipe below). Chill it for two hours or until it is set. Whip the remaining ½ cup of cream and garnish the pie with it.

BASIC PIE CRUST

2 cups all-purpose flour
Big pinch of salt
5 tablespoons unsalted butter
3 tablespoons lard or shortening
⅓ cup ice water
Flour

Combine the flour, salt, butter and lard and mix with a pastry cutter or fingers until the mixture resembles coarse meal. Then pour in just enough of the ice water to form a dough.

Divide the dough into two balls. Dust the balls in flour and wrap them in plastic wrap. Refrigerate the balls for half an hour.

Roll out each of the balls to an 11-inch circle. Place the dough in a 9-inch pie pan and crimp the edges. Makes 1 pie crust.

FOR A BAKED PIE CRUST

Preheat the oven to 375 degrees. Loosely fit aluminum foil on top of the dough and weigh the foil down with beans or pie weights. Bake for 8 to 9 minutes.

Remove the pie crust from the oven and discard the foil and beans. Prick the crust in several places with a fork. Continue baking the crust for 6 to 8 minutes more, or until lightly browned. Makes 1 pie crust.

COFFEE-EGGNOG PIE

2 eggs, separated
2 envelopes unflavored gelatin
½ cup cold coffee
2 cups hot coffee
½ cup sugar
1 tablespoon brandy
1 cup heavy cream

⅛ *teaspoon salt*
1 *square (1 ounce) unsweetened baking*
     chocolate
1 *9-inch baked pie crust (see recipe, above)*
Grated chocolate (optional, for garnish)

Beat the egg yolks well.

Soften the gelatin in the cold coffee, then dissolve it in the hot coffee. Add the sugar and stir the mixture until it is dissolved.

Pour the well-beaten egg yolks slowly into the mixture and chill it until it starts to thicken. Add the brandy.

Whip the cream and fold it into the mixture. Beat the egg whites and the salt together and fold them in. Spoon the filling into the baked pie crust and chill it until it is set. Garnish the pie with the grated chocolate. Serves 8.

COFFEE PECAN PIE

3 *eggs, beaten*
¾ *cup unsulfured molasses*
¾ *cup light corn syrup*
½ *cup double-strength coffee*
2 *tablespoons butter, melted*
¼ *teaspoon salt*
1 *teaspoon vanilla extract*
1 *cup chopped pecan meats*
4 *tablespoons flour*
1 *9-inch unbaked pie shell (see recipe, page*
     157)
whipped cream (optional, for garnish)

Preheat oven to 375 degrees.

Combine the eggs, molasses, corn syrup, coffee, melted butter, salt and vanilla and mix them thoroughly.

In another bowl, combine the pecans and flour, add this to the liquid mixture and pour it into the unbaked pie shell. Bake the pie 40 to 45 minutes, or until it is firm.

Cool the pie before cutting. Garnish it with whipped cream if desired. Since the pie is very rich, the portions should be smaller than average. Serves 7.

COFFEE MACAROON PIE

3 eggs, separated
¼ teaspoon salt
1½ cups sugar
¼ cup cold coffee
2 tablespoons butter, melted
1 teaspoon almond extract
1½ cups shredded coconut
1 unbaked 9-inch pie crust (see recipe, page
    157)

Preheat the oven to 375 degrees.

Beat the egg whites until stiff. In another bowl, add the salt to the egg yolks and beat them until they are thick and lemon colored. Add the sugar, ½ cup at a time, beating well after each addition. Add the coffee, butter and almond extract. Blend all the ingredients well, then fold in the coconut and stiffly beaten egg whites.

Turn this filling into the unbaked pie crust and bake the pie for 50 minutes, or until a knife inserted in the center comes out clean. Cool the pie before serving. Serves 8.

FUDGY COFFEE PUDDING CAKE

1 cup flour
2 teaspoons baking powder
Dash of salt
¾ cup sugar
1 heaping tablespoon unsweetened cocoa
    powder
2 teaspoons oil
1 egg
½ cup whole milk
½ teaspoon vanilla extract
¾ cup brown sugar
¼ cup unsweetened cocoa powder
½ cup chopped nuts or raisins
1¾ cups coffee, at room temperature

Preheat the oven to 350 degrees and grease a 9-inch square pan.

In a medium bowl, mix the flour, baking powder, salt and sugar. Add the tablespoon of cocoa, oil and egg, and mix them well. Add the milk and vanilla and blend well. Pour the batter into the greased pan.

In a small bowl, mix the brown sugar, the ¼ cup of cocoa and the nuts or raisins. Sprinkle this mixture over the batter, then pour the coffee over the topping and batter. Do not stir it.

Bake the cake for 40 minutes. Serve warm or at room temperature. Serves 6 to 8.

Mocha Cheesecake

1½ cups finely crushed vanilla wafers
2 tablespoons melted unsalted butter
2 tablespoons sugar
6 1-ounce squares semisweet chocolate
1½ pounds (3 8-ounce packages) cream cheese
1¼ cups sugar
3 large eggs
1 cup heavy cream
1 teaspoon vanilla extract
⅓ cup strong cooled coffee
Whipped cream (for garnish)
Grated chocolate (for garnish)

To make the crust, combine the crushed vanilla wafers, unsalted butter and the 2 tablespoons of sugar and press into the bottom and sides of a 9-inch springform pan.

Preheat the oven to 325 degrees. Melt the chocolate in the top of a double boiler over hot but not boiling water. In a large mixing bowl, beat the cream cheese and the 1¼ cups of sugar together until they are fluffy. Add the eggs, one at a time, beating thoroughly after each addition. Slowly add the cream, then the vanilla and the coffee.

Pour the melted chocolate into the cheese mixture and mix to combine the ingredients. Pour the batter into the pan and bake it for 1 hour, or until the cheesecake is set.

Cool the cake to room temperature and then chill it for at least 3 hours in the refrigerator. The cheesecake can then be garnished with whipped cream rosettes and grated chocolate if desired. Serves 8.

MOCHA FLUFF TORTE

TORTE

3 squares (3 ounces) unsweetened baking
    chocolate
¾ cup strong hot coffee
½ cup light corn syrup
1¾ cup sifted cake flour
3 teaspoons baking powder
¼ teaspoon salt
½ cup (1 stick) butter
1 cup sugar
3 eggs
1 teaspoon vanilla extract

FROSTING

6 ounces semisweet chocolate chips
¼ cup coffee
¾ cup light corn syrup
3 egg yolks, well beaten
1 cup (2 sticks) butter
2 teaspoons vanilla extract

Preheat the oven to 350 degrees. Grease two 9-inch layer cake pans and line the bottoms with wax paper. To make the torte, melt the chocolate with the hot coffee and add the light corn syrup. Stir it until the mixture thickens. Remove it from the heat and cool.

Sift the cake flour, baking powder and salt together. Set it aside. Blend the butter and sugar in a mixing bowl, then add the eggs one at a time, blending all the ingredients until they are smooth. Add the vanilla.

Stir a small amount of the sifted flour into the egg mixture. Then stir in a small amount of the cold chocolate mixture. Continue to alternate adding the two, mixing the batter smooth after each addition, and ending with the flour.

Pour the batter into the prepared pans and bake the cakes for about 35 minutes or until a cake tester or tooth-pick inserted into the center comes out clean.

Prepare the frosting by melting the chocolate chips and the coffee in the top of a double boiler over boiling water. Remove the chocolate from over the boiling water and allow it to cool.

Cook the ¾ cup of light corn syrup over medium heat until its temperature reaches 230 degrees on a candy ther-mometer, or until it spins a thread when dropped from a fork or spoon. Beating constantly, slowly add the syrup to the beaten egg yolks. Continue beating the eggs until they are thick and creamy. Blend in the butter, vanilla and cooled chocolate. Beat the frosting until fluffy, then chill it as the cakes cool.

Split each cake layer in half lengthwise to make four thin layers; spread the frosting between each. Then frost the top and sides of the torte completely. Serves 6.

COFFEE KÜCHEN

3 cups sifted flour
3 teaspoons baking powder
Dash of salt
2 cups brown sugar, firmly packed
½ cup shortening
½ cup (1 stick) butter
½ cup strong coffee
½ cup evaporated milk
⅛ teaspoon baking soda
2 eggs, beaten
1 teaspoon cinnamon

Preheat the oven to 375 degrees.

Mix the flour, baking powder, salt and brown sugar to-gether. Cut in the shortening and the butter using two knives or a pastry blender. Measure out 1 cup of this mixture and set it aside for the topping.

"The Wetter, the Better. Even the granite basin before the Old Museum must serve the Berlin nursemaids in their rage for coffee." A cartoon of the 1850s.

In another bowl, combine the coffee, evaporated milk and baking soda. Add this to the flour mixture not set aside, and mix well. Add the beaten eggs. Spoon the batter into a large muffin pan, filling each muffin cup half full. Add the cinnamon to the reserved topping mixture and sprinkle on top of the batter. Bake for 25 minutes. Makes 1 dozen.

COFFEE SNACK CAKE

2 cups flour
1 teaspoon baking powder
½ teaspoon baking soda
Dash of salt
¼ teaspoon allspice
¼ teaspoon ground cloves
¼ teaspoon nutmeg
¼ teaspoon ground ginger
½ cup chopped pecans or walnuts
½ cup (1 stick) butter
¼ cup brown sugar

½ cup honey
3 eggs
½ cup coffee
Confectioners' sugar

Preheat the oven to 350 degrees and grease a 9-inch square pan.

Sift together the flour, baking powder, baking soda, salt and spices. Add the nuts and mix well. In another bowl, cream the butter, then add the sugar, honey and eggs and mix them well. Alternately add the flour mixture and the coffee to the sugar mixture.

Pour the batter into the greased pan and bake it for 35 to 45 minutes. Cool the cake in the pan for 5 minutes, then dust it with confectioners' sugar. Serves 6.

Manhattan Ocean Club Cake

12 ounces bittersweet chocolate
2 cups very strong coffee
¾ cup (1½ sticks) unsalted butter
6 eggs, separated
1½ cups toasted macadamia nuts
¼ cup sugar
¾ cup sifted flour
Pinch of salt

ICING

8 ounces bittersweet chocolate
½ cup plus 2 tablespoons (1¼ sticks) unsalted
        butter
1 cup coffee

Preheat the oven to 350 degrees and butter and lightly flour a 12-inch cake pan. Line the pan with wax paper and set it aside.

To prepare the cake, melt the chocolate with the coffee and the butter, stirring well. In a separate bowl, beat the egg yolks and the sugar together until they are pale yellow and fluffy. Then stir the egg yolks into the chocolate mixture.

Grind the nuts in a food processor until they form a paste. Mix a third of the chocolate mixture into the paste, get rid of any lumps, then stir the nut and chocolate paste back into the batter. Stir in the sifted flour.

Beat the egg whites with a pinch of salt until they are stiff but not dry and fold them into the batter. Pour the batter into the prepared pan and bake the cake for 25 to 30 minutes. When the cake is done, the center should remain creamy.

The cake can be sprinkled with confectioners' sugar when thoroughly cool, or iced with chocolate. To prepare the icing, melt together the bittersweet chocolate, butter and coffee until the mixture is smooth and spreadable. Ice the cake with a butter knife. Serves 10 to 12.

Donna Saurage's Mocha Raisin Cake

2 cups strong hot coffee
2 cups sugar
2 tablespoons unsweetened cocoa powder
1 cup seedless raisins, chopped
½ cup (1 stick) butter
½ teaspoon vanilla extract
2 eggs
2 cups sifted all-purpose flour
½ teaspoon baking soda
2 teaspoons baking powder
½ teaspoon salt
1 teaspoon cinnamon
1 teaspoon nutmeg
½ teaspoon ground cloves
Confectioners' sugar

Preheat the oven to 350 degrees. Grease and flour a 10 × 15 × 2-inch rectangular cake pan and set it aside.

Combine the coffee, 1 cup of the sugar, the cocoa powder and the raisins in a bowl and let the mixture stand for 10 to 15 minutes. In another bowl, cream the butter and add it gradually to the remaining cup of sugar, creaming it until it is light and fluffy. Add the vanilla.

Add the eggs to the butter mixture one at a time, beating well after each addition.

Mix and sift together the remaining ingredients. Add these dry ingredients to the batter, alternating with the coffee mixture, and stir the batter thoroughly.

Pour the batter into the greased and floured pan and bake for about 1 hour. When the cake has cooled, sprinkle it with confectioners' sugar. Cut it into 2-inch squares and serve. Makes 35 squares.

ENGLISH HONEY LOAF

2¼ cups sifted flour
1 teaspoon baking powder
1 teaspoon salt
¾ teaspoon baking soda
½ teaspoon cinnamon
½ teaspoon ground cloves
½ teaspoon allspice
¼ teaspoon ground ginger
1 cup sugar
⅓ cup shortening
2 eggs
⅓ cup honey
1½ teaspoon grated lemon rind
½ cup strong cooled coffee
½ cup chopped walnuts

Preheat the oven to 350 degrees and thoroughly grease a 9 × 5 × 3-inch pan.

Sift together the flour, baking powder, salt, baking soda, and spices.

In another bowl, add the sugar gradually to the shortening, creaming well. Blend in the eggs, beating well after each addition. Add the honey and lemon rind and mix the batter until blended. Add some of the coffee and the dry ingredients to the mixture, alternating between the two and blending well after each addition. Add the walnuts and turn the batter into the pan. Bake for 55 to 65 minutes or until a cake tester or toothpick inserted in the center comes out clean. Serves 8.

COFFEE FRUITCAKE

1½ *cups sugar*
½ *cup (1 stick) butter*
3 *eggs*
3 *cups flour*
1 *tablespoon baking powder*
1 *teaspoon salt*
1 *teaspoon ground mace*
¾ *cup whole milk*
¾ *cup strong cooled coffee*
2 *cups (1 14-ounce package) mixed candied*
    fruit
½ *cup raisins*
½ *cup chopped walnuts*
1½ *teaspoons finely grated lemon peel*
1 *teaspoon vanilla extract*
Light corn syrup

Preheat the oven to 325 degrees and grease two 8 × 2 × 4-inch loaf pans.

Beat the sugar and butter in a mixing bowl until they are well combined. Add the eggs one at a time, beating well after each addition.

In a separate bowl, stir together the flour, baking powder, salt and mace. In another bowl, stir together the milk and cooled coffee. Add a small amount of the flour mixture to the creamed butter. Then add a small amount of the coffee mixture and stir. Continue to alternate additions of the flour and the coffee, mixing well after each addition.

Reserve ¼ to ½ cup of the candied fruit for garnishing the cake. Stir in the remaining fruit, raisins, walnuts, lemon peel and vanilla into the batter. Turn it into the two greased pans and bake the cakes for 1¼ hours, or until they are done (toothpick inserted in center should come out clean). Cool them in the pans for 10 minutes, then remove them and continue cooling them on wire racks.

Heat a little corn syrup and brush it lightly over the fruitcakes. Garnish the tops with the reserved candied fruit. Makes two fruitcakes. Serves 8 to 10.

COFFEE-CHERRY CAKE

CAKE

6 tablespoons butter
⅓ cup shortening
1½ cups sugar
3 eggs
2½ cups sifted cake flour
2½ teaspoons baking powder
1 teaspoon salt
1 cup strong cooled coffee
⅓ cup cherry liqueur

FILLING

2 cups high-quality tart red or black cherry
    preserves
1 tablespoon cornstarch

TOPPING

2 cups whipped cream
2 tablespoons Kahlua liqueur

Preheat the oven to 350 degrees and grease and lightly flour two 9-inch round cake pans.

Cream together the butter, shortening and sugar in a large bowl until they are light and fluffy. Add the eggs one at a time, beating well after each addition.

Sift together the cake flour, baking powder and salt. Add a bit of the flour mixture to the butter and stir the batter until it is just blended.

Next add ¼ cup of the coffee to the batter and continue to alternate adding the flour and the coffee, stirring just until blended after each addition, until all of the coffee and flour mixture have been incorporated.

Pour the batter into the two pans and bake the cakes for 25 to 30 minutes, or until a cake tester or toothpick inserted into the center comes out clean. Cool the cakes for 10 minutes in the pans, then remove them to wire racks to cool completely.

To make the filling, heat the preserves in a small saucepan over a low flame until they become liquefied. In a small bowl, stir together the cornstarch and 2 tablespoons of water and add this a little at a time to the preserves, stirring constantly. Remove the preserves from the heat and cool completely before filling the cake.

Sprinkle half the cherry liqueur over each cooled layer of the cake. Place the bottom layer on a platter. Setting aside a few cherries for garnish, spread the remaining filling on the bottom layer. Top it with the second layer of cake.

To make the topping, whip the cream and Kahlua together. Frost the sides and top of the cake with the whipped cream and garnish it with the reserved cherries. Serves 12 to 16.

COFFEE SPICE CAKE

3½ cups sifted cake flour
3 teaspoons baking powder
¼ teaspoon baking soda
¼ teaspoon salt
¼ teaspoon ground ginger
1½ teaspoons cinnamon
¼ teaspoon ground cloves
¼ teaspoon nutmeg
¾ cup (1½ sticks) unsalted butter
1½ cups sugar, brown or white
¼ cup molasses
3 eggs, well beaten
¾ cup strong cold coffee

½ cup whipped cream
Confectioners' sugar

Preheat the oven to 350 degrees. Grease two 9-inch cake pans.

Sift the flour, baking powder, soda, salt and spices together three times. Cream the butter with the sugar until fluffy, then add the molasses and eggs and beat them thoroughly. Add the dry ingredients and the coffee to the butter mixture alternately in small amounts, beating well after each addition.

Pour the mixture into the greased pans and bake 35 to 40 minutes to make two cake layers. When the layers are completely cool, spread one of the layers with the whipped cream and top it with the other layer. Sprinkle the cake with confectioners' sugar. Serves 6.

SWISS COFFEE CREAM GATEAU

CAKE

½ cup hazelnuts
½ cup almonds, blanched
3 egg whites
1¼ cup confectioners' sugar

FILLING AND FROSTING

3 egg yolks
1 cup confectioners' sugar
4 tablespoons strong coffee
½ cup (1 stick) butter
Shaved dark chocolate (for garnish)

Put the hazelnuts on a cookie sheet in a preheated 400 degree oven for a few minutes. Then remove them and rub them with a clean and dry kitchen towel until all the skins have come off. Next lower the oven temperature to 350 degrees and place the almonds on a cookie sheet. Toast them lightly in the oven for a few minutes until they are light brown. Then grind the almonds and hazel-

Swiss ladies drinking coffee. Neuchâtel, late eighteenth century.

nuts together in a food processor or blender, being careful not to grind them so fine that they become a paste.

Turn the oven up to 375 degrees.

Beat the egg whites until they are very stiff, then add half the sugar and continue beating for a few minutes. Then fold in the remaining sugar and the ground nuts.

Grease and flour two 8-inch layer cake pans and cut some wax paper to fit the bottoms. Then insert it and grease and flour the wax paper.

Pour the batter into the prepared pans and bake at 375 degrees for 20 to 25 minutes, or until a cake tester inserted into the middle comes out clean. Remove the cakes from the pans while they are still hot and let them cool on a rack.

To prepare the filling and frosting, put the egg yolks, sugar and coffee in a double boiler. Beat the mixture over high heat until it is thick. Remove it from the heat and let it cool, stirring it from time to time.

Cream the butter until it is fluffy, then add it to the egg mixture by the spoonful while beating vigorously. Spread the filling between the cooled layers and on the top and sides of the cake. The Gateau can be served as is or sprinkled with shaved dark chocolate. Serves 6 to 8.

FRENCH MOCHA CAKE

1¾ cups sifted cake flour
¼ cup unsweetened cocoa powder
½ teaspoon salt
3 teaspoons baking powder
½ cup (1 stick) butter
1 cup sugar
6 egg yolks
¾ cup whole milk
1 teaspoon vanilla extract

FROSTING

1 cup (2 sticks) butter, softened
3 cups sifted confectioners' sugar
1 teaspoon vanilla extract
Strong coffee

Preheat the oven to 350 degrees and grease two 9-inch cake pans.

Sift together twice the flour, cocoa, salt and baking powder.

In a separate bowl, cream the butter, then add the sugar gradually. Keep the mixture light and fluffy.

In another bowl, beat the egg yolks until they are as thick as mayonnaise, about 7 minutes. Add the yolks gradually to the creamed butter, beating after each addition.

Add some of the dry ingredient mixture and some of the milk, alternating between the two and mixing well after each. Stir the vanilla in and beat well. Bake the batter in the two greased pans for 25 minutes. Cool the layers completely.

To prepare the frosting, combine the butter, confectioners' sugar and vanilla and beat well. Add strong coffee until the frosting reaches spreadable consistency. Spread over one layer, put the other layer on top, and frost the top and sides. Serves 8.

CHOCOLATE ALMOND ROLL

¼ cup (½ stick) butter
1 cup diced toasted almonds
1 cup flaked coconut
1 cup semisweet chocolate pieces
⅔ cup sweetened condensed milk
4 eggs
¾ cup sugar
½ cup flour
½ teaspoon baking powder
¼ teaspoon salt
3 tablespoons cold coffee
1 teaspoon vanilla extract
¼ teaspoon baking soda
Confectioners' sugar
Sweetened whipped cream (optional)

Preheat the oven to 375 degrees and line a 10 × 15 × 1-inch jelly roll pan with foil.

To make the filling, melt the butter in the pan and spread it evenly. Combine the almonds, coconut and ½ cup of the chocolate pieces and sprinkle the mixture over the butter. Drizzle with the sweetened condensed milk and set it aside.

Melt the remaining chocolate pieces in a double boiler over warm, not hot, water. In a large bowl, beat the eggs with the sugar until they are thick and light, about 10 minutes. Add the flour, baking powder and salt, and blend the mixture well. Stir the coffee, vanilla and baking soda into the melted chocolate. Fold this into the flour mixture, then spread it evenly into the prepared pan.

Bake for 20 minutes. Remove the pan from the oven and sift confectioners' sugar over the cake and cover it with a clean tea or dish towel. Turn the cake out onto the towel and spread the filling evenly over the cake. Roll the cake up jelly roll fashion, starting from the short side. Chill it until the filling is set, at least 1 hour. Serve the cake with whipped cream, if desired. Makes 1 10-inch roll. Serves 8 to 10.

CHOCOLATE AND COFFEE PAVÉ

4 squares (4 ounces) bittersweet chocolate
¼ cup strong coffee
¼ cup (½ stick) butter
1 cup sugar
1 egg yolk
2 cups heavy cream
1 pound coconut cookies
½ cup port wine
1 cup crushed pineapple, prunes or peaches

Grate the chocolate and mix it with the coffee in a saucepan. Place the pan over low heat, and stir until the mixture is creamy and the chocolate is melted. Remove it from the heat and allow it to cool.

Place the butter, sugar and egg yolk in a mixing bowl and beat until smooth and creamy. Add the chocolate mixture, beating constantly. Continue beating and gradually add the heavy cream.

In another bowl, mix the wine and ½ cup of water, then moisten the coconut cookies with this mixture. Line a 10-inch-square baking pan with aluminum foil. In this pan, place alternating layers of cookies, chocolate mixture and fruit. The top layer should be cookies. Store the remaining chocolate mixture and the prepared pavé in the refrigerator overnight. Before serving, unmold and invert the pavé and top it with the remaining chocolate mixture. Serves 8.

Token from The Sultaness Coffee House in Sweetings Rents, Cornhill

COFFEE ICEBOX CAKE

2 cups marshmallows
1 cup strong hot coffee
1½ pints heavy cream, whipped
1 cup chopped nuts
24 ladyfinger cookies
Candied cherries (for garnish)

Melt the marshmallows in a double boiler with the hot coffee and let the mixture cool. Gently fold ⅔ of the whipped cream and all the nuts into the marshmallow. Line a 9-inch springmold or wax-paper-lined pan with some of the ladyfingers and pour a little of the marshmallow mixture over this. Add another layer of ladyfingers and continue to alternate ladyfingers with the mixture until all of it is used.

Let the cake stand in the refrigerator overnight, or at least for a few hours.

To serve, turn it out of the mold and cover it with the remaining whipped cream. Garnish the cake with the cherries. Serves 10 to 12.

COFFEE CHARLOTTE

12 ladyfinger cookies, split lengthwise
4 tablespoons strong coffee
Pinch of salt
⅔ cup sugar
2 envelopes unflavored gelatin
2¾ cups whole milk
¼ cup brandy
2 cups heavy cream, whipped
Grated bittersweet chocolate (for garnish)

Line a 9-inch springform pan along the bottom and up the sides with the ladyfingers split side facing in. Combine the coffee, salt, sugar and gelatin in a saucepan, then add the milk and stir it over low heat until the sugar and gelatin dissolve. Remove the saucepan from the heat and add the brandy.

Chill the mixture until it has stiffened slightly, then fold in the whipped cream. Pour the mixture into the lined pan and chill it for several hours, until it has set.

Unmold the charlotte by releasing the spring on the pan and garnish it with grated chocolate. Serves 6.

George II silver Lighthouse coffee pot

CLASSIC COFFEE MOUSSE

8 eggs
3 envelopes unflavored gelatin
⅔ cup sugar
2½ tablespoons cornstarch
2 cups whole milk
⅔ cup strong, cooled freshly brewed coffee
2 cups whipping cream

Beat the eggs well in a large bowl. Then mix the gelatin, sugar and cornstarch in a 2½-quart saucepan and stir in the milk. Stir the mixture constantly over medium heat until the gelatin dissolves and the mixture thickens and comes to a boil. Remove it from the heat.

Gradually whisk the hot mixture into the beaten eggs. Return it to the saucepan and stir it constantly over low heat for two minutes. Strain the mixture immediately into a large bowl and chill it, stirring frequently, until it is thoroughly cool.

Stir the coffee into the gelatin mixture and chill it again, stirring frequently until it is slightly thickened. Whip the cream and fold it in. Turn the mousse into a 2-quart mold and chill it until it is firm (about 2 hours).

To unmold the mousse, dip the mold up to the rim in a large bowl or sink full of warm water. Then cover the top of the mold with a plate and invert the mousse onto the plate. Serves 12.

CHOCOLATE WALNUT MOUSSE

1 package (6 ounces) semisweet chocolate bits
½ cup whole milk
2 teaspoons unflavored gelatin
2 eggs, separated
⅛ teaspoon salt
⅛ teaspoon cream of tartar
3 tablespoons sugar
¼ cup Amaretto di Saronno liqueur
1½ cups heavy cream, whipped
½ cup toasted walnuts, chopped
1 ounce semisweet chocolate, melted and
　　cooled
1 tablespoon Kahlua liqueur
Walnut halves (for garnish)

Combine the chocolate bits and milk in a saucepan over very low heat, stirring occasionally until the chocolate melts.

In a bowl, soften the gelatin in 2 tablespoons of cold water. In another bowl, beat the egg yolks slightly. Stir a little bit of the hot chocolate mixture into the egg yolks. Then pour the egg yolks into the saucepan with the rest of the chocolate mixture and cook, stirring until it thickens slightly. Do not allow the mixture to boil. Next stir the gelatin into the chocolate mixture until it is dissolved. Cool it to room temperature.

Beat the egg whites with the salt and cream of tartar until they are stiff. Gradually beat in the sugar. Stir the Amaretto into the cooled chocolate mixture. Fold in the beaten egg whites, two-thirds of the whipped cream and the chopped nuts. Turn the mousse into a 6-cup dish or serving bowl and chill it overnight.

Fold the chocolate and Kahlua into the remaining whipped cream and pipe it in rosettes to form a garnish on top of the mousse. Decorate the mousse with walnut halves. Serves 6 to 8.

COFFEE CARAMEL CUSTARD

CARAMEL

1 cup sugar
¼ teaspoon cream of tartar

CUSTARD

3 cups half-and-half
1 cup strong coffee
2 sticks cinnamon
1 teaspoon vanilla extract
6 eggs
2 egg yolks
1½ cups sugar

In a small saucepan, bring the sugar, ¼ cup of water and cream of tartar to a boil and cook until the sugar is dissolved. Turn the heat down and cook slowly without stirring until it becomes a deep golden brown. Pour the caramel into serving cups such as individual soufflé dishes or baba cups, handling the caramel carefully to avoid burns. A single large container such as a 2-quart soufflé dish or a charlotte mold may also be used. Swirl the caramel around to coat the bottom and sides of the molds. Discard any excess caramel that collects at the bottom. Then set the molds aside to cool.

Preheat the oven to 325 degrees.

To prepare the custard, combine the coffee, half-and-half and cinnamon sticks in a saucepan and bring the mixture to a boil over moderate heat. Add the vanilla.

Meanwhile, with an electric mixer, beat the eggs, egg yolks and 1½ cups of sugar until thick. Strain the coffee, milk and cinnamon stick mixture and, while the mixer is running, slowly add it to the eggs. Strain the custard again through a fine sieve into a bowl. Pour the custard into the prepared cups or container and place in a large, shallow baking pan. Place the pan on a shelf in the oven. Then pour boiling water into the pan until it reaches halfway up the sides of the custard cups or serving dish and bake about 40 to 45 minutes until set (knife inserted off-center should come out clean).

Cool completely. To unmold, dip a sharp knife in cold water and run its blade along the inside of the mold. Place a serving plate on top and turn the mold over onto the plate. Jiggle the mold gently to loosen custard, and carefully lift the mold off. Serves 8.

COFFEE FROZEN CUSTARD

¾ cup sugar
Dash of salt
½ cup strong, freshly brewed coffee
¼ cup light corn syrup
2 envelopes unflavored gelatin
2 cups instant nonfat milk powder
4 cups whole milk
1 teaspoon vanilla extract or ½ teaspoon
* brandy flavoring*

Make a coffee syrup by mixing together the sugar, salt, coffee and the corn syrup in a saucepan. Bring to a boil and boil it for 2 minutes.

In a cup, sprinkle the gelatin over ½ cup of cold water to soften it.

In a saucepan, stir the milk powder into the whole milk, blend in the softened gelatin and hot coffee syrup. Cook over low heat, stirring constantly, until the gelatin dissolves. Remove from the heat. Stir in the vanilla or brandy flavoring, then turn the mixture out of the pan and into ice cube trays and freeze until firm, but not frozen.

Beat the custard until it is smooth. Spoon it into sherbet or parfait glasses, or pipe it through a pastry tube into a decorative shape. Serves 8 to 10.

Coffee Bavarian Cream

2 egg yolks, beaten
½ cup sugar
¼ teaspoon salt
½ cup whole milk
1 envelope unflavored gelatin
½ teaspoon vanilla extract
½ cup black coffee
2 egg whites
1 cup whipping cream
Whipped cream (for garnish)
Grated sweet chocolate (for garnish)

In the top of a double boiler, mix together the egg yolks, ¼ cup of the sugar, and the salt. Slowly add the milk. Cook the mixture over hot water, stirring it constantly, until it begins to thicken.

Soften the gelatin in ¼ cup of cold water, then add it to the egg yolk mixture and stir until it is completely dissolved. Stir in the vanilla and coffee and refrigerate the mixture until slightly thickened (about 1 hour).

Beat the egg whites until stiff. Slowly add the remaining ¼ cup of sugar, beating constantly.

Whip the cream and fold it into the gelatin mixture. Then fold in the beaten egg whites. Pour the bavarian cream into 12 individual dessert cups and chill until firm. Top each with whipped cream and grated chocolate. Serves 12.

During Lebanese wedding festivities, the coffee maker is kept busy over his fire.

MOCHA POTS-DE-CRÈME

1½ cups whipping cream
½ cup strong coffee
6 ounces sweet cooking chocolate, grated
2 tablespoons sugar
6 egg yolks, slightly beaten
1 teaspoon vanilla extract

Preheat the oven to 300 degrees.

Combine the cream, coffee, chocolate and sugar in a saucepan and stir over low heat until the chocolate melts and the cream is scalded. Remove the mixture from the heat.

Pour a little of the hot mixture on the egg yolks and blend, then add the egg yolks to the chocolate mixture. Add the vanilla and mix it well. Strain the mixture into pots-de-crème or custard cups and cover them. (If custard cups are used, cover them with foil.) Set the pots or cups in a pan of warm water and bake them for 20 minutes. Uncover them and chill until serving. Serves 6.

Bread Pudding
with Coffee Hard Sauce

PUDDING

2 cups whole milk
¼ cup (4 tablespoons) unsalted butter
½ cup sugar
4 cups day-old French bread, cut into small
*   cubes*
2 eggs, beaten
Pinch of salt
¼ teaspoon freshly grated nutmeg
1 teaspoon vanilla extract

SAUCE

½ cup (1 stick) unsalted butter
1½ cups brown sugar
4 tablespoons strong hot coffee
2 tablespoons Kahlua liqueur (optional)

Preheat the oven to 350 degrees.

In a small saucepan, scald the milk and the butter, then stir in the sugar. Pour this mixture over the bread cubes and let it stand for 10 minutes. Add the beaten eggs, salt, nutmeg and vanilla. Pour the mixture into a buttered 1½-quart ovenproof dish and bake it for 35 to 40 minutes, or until a cake tester or toothpick inserted in the center comes out clean.

To prepare the sauce, cream the ½ cup of butter with the dark brown sugar. Slowly add the 4 tablespoons of hot coffee and mix well, beating if necessary to get out all the lumps. Add Kahlua and mix well.

To serve, ladle the sauce over the warm pudding. Serves 4.

ZHIVAGO

> 1 envelope unflavored gelatin
> 1 cup crème de menthe liqueur
> 1 cup strong hot coffee
> 2 teaspoons sugar
> 4 tablespoons whipped cream (for garnish)
> 4 maraschino cherries (for garnish)
> 4 mint leaves (for garnish)
> Coffee Tortoni (recipe below)

Dissolve half the envelope of gelatin in 2 tablespoons of boiling water and combine it with the crème de menthe. Pour it evenly into four parfait glasses and chill the parfaits until they are set.

Dissolve the remaining gelatin in the hot coffee. Then add the sugar and mix it well. Dividing the mixture evenly, pour it over the mint layer in the parfait glasses. Chill the parfaits again until they have set. Top each parfait with a layer of coffee tortoni (recipe follows) and chill. To serve, garnish each with a tablespoon of whipped cream, a maraschino cherry and a mint leaf. Serves 4.

A token from the coffee house Morat Ye Great in Exchange Alley

COFFEE TORTONI

1 egg white
1 tablespoon high-quality instant coffee
6 tablespoons sugar
1 cup heavy cream
2 tablespoons toasted slivered almonds

Beat the egg white until it is stiff, then mix it well with the instant coffee and 2 tablespoons of the sugar. Combine the heavy cream and the remaining 4 tablespoons of sugar, whipping it until stiff.

Combine all the ingredients, mix well and pour into four sherbet glasses (or use as the crowning layer of the Zhivago, as outlined in the preceding recipe). Chill the tortoni before serving. Serves 4.

RUSSIAN COFFEE PARFAIT

2½ cups fresh cream
½ cup freshly ground coffee
6 egg yolks
1 cup sugar
1 tablespoon unflavored gelatin
Grated bittersweet chocolate (for garnish)

Bring the cream to a boil, then add the coffee, cover and set it aside for 30 to 45 minutes.

In another bowl, blend the egg yolks and sugar together. Strain the coffee-cream and add it to the egg yolk–sugar mixture.

Dissolve the gelatin in ½ cup of warm water and pour it in, mixing well.

Rinse out a 5-cup mold with cold water, pour in the coffee cream and put it in the refrigerator or freezer until it is set (about 1 hour).

Unmold the parfait by dipping the mold up to the rim in a bowl of hot water. Place a serving platter or dish on top, and invert the parfait onto the platter. Garnish with the chocolate. Serves 8.

FAIRMONT COFFEE ICE CREAM

10 egg yolks
1½ cups sugar
6 tablespoons high-quality instant coffee
2 cups whole milk
1 pint heavy cream
¼ cup Kahlua liqueur

Combine the egg yolks, sugar and instant coffee powder in a mixing bowl, then whip them together into a fluffy mousse.

Bring the milk just to a boil and pour it over the mousse, stirring it constantly. Cook the mixture over low heat until it coats the back of a spoon. Set it aside to cool.

When the mixture is cool, add the heavy cream and Kahlua, then prepare the ice cream in an ice cream maker according to the manufacturer's instructions. Makes 1½ quarts, at least 20 servings.

FROZEN CAPPUCCINO

1 package unflavored gelatin
1½ cups cold coffee
⅔ cup sugar
1 ounce semisweet chocolate, cut in half
1 cup hot coffee
1 cup heavy cream
2–3 tablespoons coffee liqueur

Sprinkle the gelatin over ½ cup of the cold coffee in a small saucepan and let it stand for 5 minutes. Place the sugar and chocolate in the work bowl of a food processor and process using the metal blade. Pulse two or three times, then process the mixture continuously for 1 minute until the chocolate is finely chopped. Leave the chocolate in the food processor.

Stir the gelatin mixture over low heat for 2 minutes, or until it dissolves. With the food processor running, pour the gelatin mixture and the hot coffee through the feed

A London coffee house in the eighteenth century

tube. Process the mixture until the chocolate melts—about 15 seconds. Then transfer it to a 2-quart bowl and stir in the remaining cold coffee and the cream. Pour it into a 9 × 9 × 2-inch pan. Then cover it and freeze it until solid.

Cut the frozen mixture into 1-inch cubes and spoon them into the food processor. Process the mixture with the metal blade, pulsing 2 or 3 times, then process continuously until it is smooth—about 1 minute. Scrape the bowl as necessary. With the machine running, pour the liqueur through the feed tube and process for 3 seconds. Transfer the mixture back to the 2-quart bowl. Cover it and freeze it for 1 to 2 hours until it is almost firm. Serve it in chilled dessert dishes. Makes about 1 quart.

COFFEE WALNUT SAUCE

1 cup sugar
1½ cups strong coffee
2 tablespoons cornstarch

3 tablespoons cold coffee
2 tablespoons butter
⅓ teaspoon salt
½ cup broken walnut meats

Melt the sugar slowly in a heavy skillet, stirring often. Add the 1½ cups of coffee slowly and carefully (much steam will rise). Stir the sauce constantly.

Dissolve the cornstarch in the cold coffee, then stir into the warm sauce and continue stirring it over low heat until the sauce boils and thickens. Add the butter, salt and walnuts. Serve the sauce warm over ice cream. Makes about 2 cups.

CREAM PUFFS
WITH COFFEE-RUM SAUCE

PUFFS

1 cup (2 sticks) butter
⅛ teaspoon salt
2 cups all-purpose flour
8 eggs

CREAM

2 cups heavy cream, whipped
4 tablespoons strong cold coffee
Sugar

COFFEE-RUM SAUCE

1 cup sugar
1½ cups strong coffee
3 tablespoons cold coffee
2 tablespoons cornstarch
2 tablespoons butter
2 tablespoons rum

Preheat the oven to 400 degrees and lightly grease a cookie sheet or a baking pan.

To prepare the puffs, boil 1 cup of water in a saucepan, add the butter and salt and stir. Reduce the heat and add the flour, beating the mixture until it pulls away from the sides of the pan and forms a smooth ball in the center. Remove it from the heat and add the eggs, one at a time, beating well after each addition.

Using a dessert spoon, shape the puffs into 1½-inch balls and place them on the lightly greased baking pan or cookie sheet. Bake them for 8 minutes. Then reduce the heat to 350 degrees and bake them for an additional 10 to 12 minutes.

To make the cream, add the coffee slowly to the whipped cream, folding it in well. Sweeten it to taste. When the puffs have cooled, cut off their tops and fill them with this coffee cream. Replace the tops. Chill.

The coffee-rum sauce is prepared by melting the sugar in a saucepan over low heat, stirring constantly. Gradually add the strong coffee, stirring constantly until the sugar is completely dissolved. Mix the cold coffee with the cornstarch and combine it with the heated mixture. Cook the combined ingredients until they boil and thicken, then remove them from the heat. Add the butter and rum, stirring until the butter melts. Pour the coffee-rum sauce over the cream puffs. Serves 8.

NEWPORT CLIPPER COOKIES

1⅔ cups brown sugar
1½ cups (3 sticks) butter
1½ teaspoons baking soda
1½ teaspoons salt
2 tablespoons freshly brewed coffee
1 tablespoon vanilla extract
3 large eggs
4½ cups pastry flour
1½ cups semisweet chocolate chips
¾ cup macadamia nuts, chopped

Preheat the oven to 350 degrees.

Cream the sugar and butter together well in a large mixing bowl. Add the baking soda, salt, coffee and vanilla and mix them thoroughly. Add the eggs, mix, then add the pastry flour to form a smooth dough.

Fold in the chocolate chips and macadamia nuts. Drop the dough by the tablespoon onto a greased cookie sheet and bake the cookies until they are brown around the edges. Makes about 3 dozen cookies.

COFFEE BRANDY COOKIES

½ cup shortening
¾ cup sugar
2 eggs, beaten well
¼ cup strong coffee
½ teaspoon brandy flavoring
1½ cups sifted flour
1½ teaspoons baking powder
¼ teaspoon salt
2 cups wheat flakes

Preheat the oven to 400 degrees and grease a cookie sheet.

Cream together the shortening and sugar, then add the well-beaten eggs and mix everything thoroughly. Stir in the coffee and the flavoring.

In another bowl, mix and sift the flour, baking powder and salt. Add this to the coffee mixture and stir it until smooth. Crush the wheat flakes slightly, form teaspoonfuls of the cookie mixture into balls and roll them in the flakes. Place the cookies on a greased cookie sheet, 2 inches apart. Bake 12 minutes. Makes 3½ dozen cookies.

COFFEE DATE BARS

FILLING

1 cup chopped dates, raisins or figs
¾ cup sugar
½ cup coffee
Grated zest of 1 lemon

BARS

1 cup (2 sticks) butter, melted
1 cup brown sugar
½ cup coffee
2 cups flour
1 teaspoon baking soda
1 cup oatmeal

To prepare the filling, combine all the filling ingredients in a saucepan and stir them over medium heat until the fruit is tender and the mixture is thick and smooth. Cool it to room temperature.

Preheat the oven to 325 degrees and grease a 12 × 8-inch pan. To make the bars, combine the butter, sugar and coffee in a large bowl. In another bowl, combine the dry ingredients and add them to the butter-sugar mixture. Beat it well. Spread half the bar batter on the bottom of the greased pan. Cover it with the filling, then spread the rest of the batter on top. Bake for 40 to 45 minutes. Let the cake cool before cutting it into two-inch-square bars. Makes 35 bars.

COFFEE TOFFEE SQUARES

1 cup chocolate wafer crumbs
2 tablespoons butter, melted
½ cup (1 stick) butter
¾ cup sugar
4 eggs, separated
1 square (1 ounce) unsweetened chocolate,
*   melted and cooled*
2 teaspoons high-quality instant coffee
*   powder*
½ teaspoon vanilla extract
2¼ ounces chocolate-covered toffee candy

Combine the crumbs and the melted butter and press the mixture into the bottom of an 8-inch square baking pan to form the crust. Cream together the stick of butter and ½ cup of the sugar until they are light and fluffy.

Thoroughly beat in the egg yolks, chocolate, coffee powder and vanilla.

In another bowl, beat the egg whites until soft peaks form. Gradually add the remaining ¼ cup sugar, beating the egg whites until stiff peaks form. Fold the egg white mixture into the chocolate mixture. Spread this over the crust. Coarsely crush the toffee bars and sprinkle them over the chocolate mixture. Freeze the mixture until firm, 3 to 4 hours, and cut into squares. Makes 25 squares.

MOCHA BALLS

1 large (7-ounce) box vanilla wafers
2 cups confectioners' sugar
⅔ cups finely chopped pecans or walnuts
2 tablespoons unsweetened cocoa powder
¼ cup heavy cream
¼ cup cold strong coffee
Confectioners' sugar

Crush the vanilla wafers into fine crumbs: there should be 2 cups. Add the sugar and mix well, then stir in the nutmeats and cocoa. Add the cream and coffee. Mix well and shape the mixture into balls about ¾ inch in diameter. Roll the balls in additional confectioners' sugar. Chill the balls until cold, about 1 hour. Makes about 4 dozen balls.

COFFEE BRIGADEIROS

1 14-ounce can sweetened condensed milk
1 tablespoon unsweetened cocoa powder
⅓ cup strong coffee
1 tablespoon butter
½ cup grated coconut

Butter or grease a plate.
Mix all the ingredients except the coconut in a sauce-

pan. Cook them over low heat until the mixture becomes clear and it pulls away from the sides of the pan. Pour the mixture onto the greased plate and allow it to cool.

Wet your hands and shape the mixture into little balls. Roll the balls in the grated coconut. Makes 2 dozen balls.

COFFEE TRUFFLES

1 cup finely chopped walnuts
1 cup vanilla wafer cookie crumbs
1 cup chocolate chips
½ cup strong coffee
2 tablespoons Kahlua liqueur
½ cup unsweetened cocoa powder
½ cup confectioners' sugar

In a saucepan, combine the nuts, cookie crumbs, chocolate chips, coffee and Kahlua. Stir the mixture over low heat until the chocolate melts. Cool it to room temperature and then chill until the chocolate is firm, about 40 minutes.

In a shallow bowl, mix the cocoa powder and confectioners' sugar. Scoop the chocolate up with a teaspoon or melon baller and, working quickly, form it into 1-inch balls with your fingers. Roll each ball in the cocoa and place it on a cookie sheet. Refrigerate the truffles until 30 minutes before serving. Makes 72 truffles.

COFFEE WALNUTS

1½ cups chopped walnuts
1 cup packed brown sugar
½ cup sugar
½ cup light cream
1 tablespoon high-quality instant coffee
1 teaspoon vanilla extract

Preheat the oven to 350 degrees.

Line a 9 × 5 × 3-inch loaf pan with foil, extending the foil over the edges. Butter the foil.

Spread the walnuts in a single layer in a shallow baking pan and toast them for 10 minutes in the oven, stirring them occasionally. Keep the walnuts warm.

Butter the sides of a heavy 1½-quart saucepan. In the pan, combine the brown sugar, white sugar, cream and instant coffee. Cook and stir the sugars over high heat until the mixture is boiling. Clip a candy thermometer to the pan. Lower the flame to medium heat, stirring frequently, until the thermometer registers 236 degrees, the soft-ball stage. Remove the pan from the heat. Remove the thermometer.

Add the vanilla. Beat it gently for 2 minutes, then stir in the walnuts. Turn into the prepared loaf pan and cool the mixture for 10 minutes. Use the foil to lift the candy out of the pan. Cut it into 1½-inch strips, then cut the strips into 1½-inch triangles. Makes about 36 pieces.

BANANA FRITTERS WITH COFFEE-RUM SAUCE

SAUCE

1 cup sugar
1½ cups strong hot coffee
2 tablespoons cornstarch
3 tablespoons cold coffee
2 tablespoons butter
2 tablespoons rum

FRITTERS

1 cup flour, sifted
2 teaspoons baking powder
1¼ teaspoons salt
¼ cup sugar
1 egg, well beaten
⅓ cup whole milk
2 teaspoons melted shortening
2 or 3 firm bananas
Additional flour

To prepare the coffee-rum sauce, melt the sugar in a pan over low heat, stirring it often. Add the hot coffee slowly, stirring constantly. In a bowl, blend the cornstarch and cold coffee, then stir it into the sugar-coffee mixture. Continue to cook and stir until the sauce boils and thickens. Remove it from the heat. Add the butter and rum and stir the sauce until the butter dissolves. Set the sauce aside and keep it warm until the fritters are ready.

To make the fritters, mix and sift the flour, baking powder, salt and sugar. In another bowl, combine the egg, milk and melted shortening, then add this mixture to the dry ingredients and mix until the batter is smooth. The batter should be stiff—do not thin it out.

Cut each banana into 3 or 4 equal pieces. Roll these in flour, then dip them into the fritter batter to coat. Fry the bananas in shallow fat (2 inches deep) for about 5 minutes. Turn them often to brown them evenly, then drain them on a rack.

Serve the sauce over the hot banana fritters. Serves 4.

A woman coffee seller, about 1730

Great with Coffee

FRENCH MARKET BEIGNETS

1 cup whole milk
1 tablespoon shortening
2 tablespoons sugar
1 package (2 teaspoons) dry yeast
3 cups all-purpose flour
1 teaspoon nutmeg
1 teaspoon salt
1 egg
Oil for deep frying
Confectioners' sugar (for garnish)

Heat the milk over a low flame to the scalding point, stirring it constantly.

Place the shortening and sugar in a bowl and add the hot milk, stirring the mixture until the sugar is dissolved and the shortening is melted. Allow the mixture to cool to lukewarm, then add the yeast and stir until it is completely dissolved.

Sift the flour, nutmeg and salt together and gradually add about half of this mixture to the milk to form a batter. When the batter is smooth, add the egg and beat it in until it is well blended. Add the rest of the flour mixture to the batter and stir until it is smooth. Cover the bowl with a towel and set the batter aside to rise.

The dough will approximately double in volume in about 1 hour. Place the dough on a floured board and knead it gently. Then roll it out to a thickness of one-quarter inch. Cut the dough into diamond shapes with a sharp knife and cover them with a towel for 45 minutes.

Heat the oil to 385 degrees, checking the temperature with a thermometer. Fry the beignets; try to turn them only once. When they are golden brown, drain them on a paper towel and dust them with confectioners' sugar. Makes 2 dozen.

Brennan's Bananas Foster

¼ cup (½ stick) butter
1 cup brown sugar
½ teaspoon cinnamon
4 tablespoons banana liqueur
4 bananas, cut in half lengthwise, then
*   halved*
¼ cup rum
4 scoops good-quality vanilla ice cream

Melt the butter over an alcohol burner in a flambé pan or an attractive skillet. Add the sugar, cinnamon and banana liqueur, stirring until they are mixed. Heat for a few minutes, then place the quartered bananas in the sauce and sauté them until they are soft and slightly browned.

Add the rum and allow it to heat well, then tip the pan so that the flame from the burner causes the sauce to ignite. Allow the sauce to flame until it dies out, tipping the pan with a circular motion to prolong the pyrotechnics.

Serve the bananas over the vanilla ice cream, then spoon the hot sauce from the pan over the top. Serves 4.

Antoine's Baked Alaska

1 10-ounce pound cake
7 large egg whites, at room temperature
¼ teaspoon salt
1 cup sugar
1 quart good-quality vanilla ice cream,
*   softened*

Cut the cake into ½-inch-thick slices. Whip the egg whites with the salt until they reach the soft-peak stage. Gradually whip in ¾ cup of the sugar until it is completely dissolved and the whites stand in stiff peaks. Set it aside.

Line the bottom of a 12-inch oval ovenproof pan with some of the cake slices, cutting some into smaller pieces to fit. Scoop the ice cream onto the cake and form it into a half-rounded football shape, leaving an uncovered border of cake 1 inch around the edge of the pan. Pack the ice cream scoops hard together and cover them with the remaining cake slices and pieces. Place in the freezer to harden.

When ready to serve, preheat the oven to 500 degrees and remove the cake-covered ice cream from the freezer. Reserving one cup of the whipped egg whites for decoration, ice the cake by applying the rest of the egg whites smoothly with a spoon or spatula. Be sure to bring the egg whites over the cake border and well onto the pan.

Return the cake to the freezer. Whip again the reserved cup of egg whites with the remaining ¼ cup of sugar, making sure all grains are dissolved. Turn the mixture into a pastry bag that has been fitted with a small nozzle and set aside. Remove the Alaska from the freezer and brown it in the preheated oven for only 2 to 3 minutes.

Decorate the Alaska with the remaining egg white–sugar mixture by adding piping or writing and serve it immediately. The Alaska should be taken to the table whole and scooped onto small plates. Serves 6 to 8.

CARIBBEAN ROOM
MILE-HIGH ICE CREAM PIE

CRUST

1½ cups sifted flour
½ teaspoon salt
½ cup shortening

FILLING

*1 pint good-quality vanilla ice cream, slightly
    softened*
*1 pint good-quality chocolate ice cream,
    slightly softened*
*1 pint good-quality peppermint ice cream,
    slightly softened*
8 egg whites
½ teaspoon vanilla extract

¼ teaspoon cream of tartar
½ cup sugar

CHOCOLATE SAUCE

6 squares (6 ounces) German sweet chocolate
6 squares (6 ounces) unsweetened chocolate
1½ cups sugar
1½ cups heavy cream

Preheat the oven to 450 degrees.

To make the crust, sift together the flour and salt. Cut the shortening into the flour-salt mixture until the pieces are the size of small peas. Sprinkle 1 teaspoon of cold water over the flour mixture and gently toss with a fork. Repeat until the dough is moistened, using 4 or 5 tablespoons of cold water in all.

Form the dough into a ball and roll it out on a lightly floured surface to a thickness of one-eighth inch. Fit the crust loosely into a 9-inch pie pan, pricking well with a fork. Bake the crust for 10 to 12 minutes. Set the crust aside to cool.

Layer the slightly softened ice cream in the cooled pie shell.

George III silver coffee pot

Beat the egg whites with the vanilla and the cream of tartar until soft peaks form. Gradually add the ½ cup of sugar, beating until the egg whites are stiff and glossy and the sugar has dissolved. Spread the meringue over the ice cream to the edges of the pastry.

Place the pie under the broiler for 30 seconds to 1 minute to brown the meringue, then freeze it for several hours.

To prepare the chocolate sauce, place the chocolates, the sugar and ¾ cup of the heavy cream in the top of a double boiler. Cook the sauce until it is melted and thick, then add the remaining cream to achieve a pouring consistency. Drizzle the hot chocolate sauce over each slice. Serves 6 to 8.

CABLE BEACH COFFEE CAKE

CAKE

1½ packages (1 tablespoon) dry yeast
1 cup whole milk
6 tablespoons sugar
1½ teaspoons salt
1 egg
Grated rind of 1 lemon
4 cups bread flour
¼ cup (½ stick) butter
Melted butter
Crushed almonds or confectioners' sugar
      (optional)

FILLING

2½ cups ground hazelnuts or almonds
1⅛ cups sugar
3 egg whites

TOPPING

5 ounces dark unsweetened chocolate
5 eggs, separated
5 tablespoons sugar

Grated rind of 1 orange
2 tablespoons Cointreau liqueur
½ cup heavy cream
Chocolate shavings or orange sections
(optional, for garnish)

Grease a large baking pan (so that braids can keep their form) and set it aside.

To make the cake, dissolve the dry yeast in the milk, then add the sugar, salt and egg. Stir it until the sugar is dissolved. Add the grated lemon rind and flour, mixing it until it becomes a paste. Work the 4 tablespoons of butter into the paste until it forms a smooth dough. Set the dough aside, uncovered, for 30 minutes.

To prepare the filling, mix the nuts and sugar with the egg whites until they are fluffy. Set the filling aside.

Cut the dough in half, and roll out each half into a square one-quarter inch thick. Spread the filling evenly on both of the squares and roll them up. Cut each roll lengthwise and braid the two halves together, with the cut side facing up.

Place the braids on the greased baking pan and let them stand at room temperature for 15 minutes, while preheating the oven to 350 degrees.

Bake the braids for 25 minutes. Remove the cakes from the oven and brush them with melted butter. After the two coffee cakes have cooled, sprinkle them with crushed almonds or confectioners' sugar.

To prepare the chocolate cream topping, cut the chocolate into small squares and melt it in a small saucepan over low heat. Whip together the egg yolks and sugar and add the warm liquid chocolate. Add the grated orange rind and the Cointreau.

Whip the egg whites and mix them in, then place the topping in the refrigerator to cool. Before serving, whip the heavy cream and mix it in. Place the mixture in a serving bowl, decorating it with chocolate shavings or orange sections. The bowl of topping should be served with the cake. Serves 8.

ORANGE-BUTTER COFFEE CAKE

CAKE

1 package (2 teaspoons) active dry yeast
2 beaten eggs
½ cup sour cream
6 tablespoons butter, melted
¼ cup sugar
1 teaspoon salt
2¾–3¼ cups all-purpose flour

FILLING

2 tablespoons butter, melted
¾ cup sugar
¾ cup flaked coconut
2 teaspoons grated orange peel

GLAZE

¼ cup sugar
½ cup sour cream
¼ cup orange juice
¼ cup (½ stick) butter

TOPPING

¼ cup flaked coconut

In a mixing bowl, dissolve the yeast in ¼ cup warm water. Allow to stand until foamy, about 5 minutes. Stir in the eggs, sour cream, the 6 tablespoons of butter, ¼ cup sugar and salt. Then stir in 2¾ cups of the flour.

Turn the dough out onto a lightly floured surface and knead in enough of the remaining flour to make a moderately soft dough that is smooth and elastic. Place the dough in a greased bowl, turning it once to coat it, and cover it with a towel. Let the dough rise until it doubles in bulk, about 1½ hours.

Punch the dough down. Turn it out onto a lightly floured surface and divide it in half. Shape each half into a ball, then cover the balls and let them rest for 10 minutes. Meanwhile, grease two 9-inch round cake pans.

Roll each ball into a 12-inch circle. Brush each with 1 tablespoon of melted butter.

In a bowl, combine the ¾ cup sugar, ¾ cup coconut and orange peel and sprinkle this mixture over the circles. Cut each circle into 12 wedges and roll them up, starting at the wide ends.

Arrange the rolls, pinwheel fashion, in the two greased pans. Preheat the oven to 350 degrees. Cover the rolls and let them rise until they double in bulk, about 30 minutes.

Bake the cakes for 25 to 30 minutes, then remove them immediately from the pans. Place the coffee cakes on wire racks over waxed paper.

To make the glaze, combine the sugar, sour cream, orange juice and butter in a saucepan. Stir the mixture over medium heat until the sugar dissolves, then bring it to a boil. Boil the glaze for 3 minutes, stirring constantly.

Let the glaze cool a little, then top the cooled cakes with the glaze and sprinkle them with the remaining ¼ cup of coconut. Makes 2 cakes. Each cake serves 8.

BRAN-APPLE COFFEE CAKE

CAKE

3 cups whole bran cereal
1½ cups sugar
⅓ cup (5 tablespoons plus one teaspoon)
    butter
2 eggs
1 cup buttermilk
1 cup applesauce
2½ cups all-purpose flour
2½ teaspoons baking soda
½ teaspoon salt

TOPPING

1 cup all-purpose flour
½ cup packed brown sugar
1 teaspoon cinnamon
½ cup (1 stick) butter

Preheat the oven to 400 degrees and grease two 9 × 9 × 2-inch baking pans. To make the cake, combine 1 cup of the cereal with 1 cup of boiling water and set it aside.

Cream the sugar and butter together, then beat in the eggs. Stir in the buttermilk, applesauce and water-softened bran.

In a medium mixing bowl, stir together the 2½ cups of flour, the baking soda and the salt. Add the 2 cups remaining cereal and the egg mixture, combining all ingredients well. Pour the batter into the two greased pans.

For the topping, combine the cup of flour, brown sugar and cinnamon. Cut in the butter, then sprinkle half the topping mixture onto each coffee cake. Bake for 30 to 35 minutes. Serve them warm or cold. Makes two coffee cakes, each cake serving 8.

GRANDMOTHER'S COFFEE CAKE

CAKE

1½ *packages (1 tablespoon) active dry yeast*
1¾ *cups whole milk*
½ *cup (1 stick) butter*
6¾ *cups all-purpose flour*
1½ *teaspoons salt*
1½ *cups raisins*
1 *cup plus 2 tablespoons sugar*
2 *eggs, beaten*

TOPPING

½ *cup sugar*
½ *cup all-purpose flour*
¼ *cup (½ stick) butter, at room temperature*
½ *cup chopped walnuts*
1 *egg, beaten*
Cinnamon

Oil a large bowl. In another large bowl, sprinkle the yeast over ¼ cup of warm water. Let it stand until it has dissolved, then stir it to blend.

Coffee house, 1848

Heat the milk and butter in a small saucepan over low heat until the butter is soft but not completely melted, about 2 minutes. Blend this mixture into the yeast. Sift together the flour and salt. *Add 1 cup of the flour* to the yeast mixture. Blend in ½ cup of the raisins. Mix in 6 tablespoons of the sugar and one-third of the beaten eggs.

Repeat the directions from *Add 1 cup of flour* twice more. At this point, 3 cups of the flour and all of the raisins, sugar and eggs should be incorporated into the dough. Beat in the remaining flour.

Transfer the dough to the oiled bowl, turning it once to coat it and cover it with a towel. Let the dough rise in a warm, draft-free area until it has doubled in volume, 3 to 4 hours.

To prepare the topping, blend the sugar, flour and butter in a medium bowl, using a pastry blender or two knives until the mixture is crumbly. Stir in the chopped walnuts and set it aside.

Grease two cookie sheets. Punch the dough down and divide it into five pieces. Then form each piece into a 6 × 4-inch oval. Transfer the ovals to the prepared cookie sheets. Brush the loaves with the beaten egg and press half the topping onto the tops of the loaves. Cover the loaves with towels and let them rise again until they have almost doubled in bulk, about 1½ hours.

Preheat the oven to 275 degrees. Press the remaining topping onto the loaves. Sprinkle them with cinnamon and bake them until they are lightly golden, about 40 minutes. Cool them and wrap them airtight. Store the cakes at room temperature or freeze them for up to a month. Makes five cakes. Each cake serves 3.

German Apple Pancake

2 tablespoons sugar
1 teaspoon cinnamon
2 tablespoons butter
2 large cooking apples, peeled, cored and cut into ¼-inch slices
⅓ cup raisins
¼ cup apple brandy, apple cider or apple juice
3 eggs
½ cup all-purpose flour
½ cup whole milk
½ teaspoon salt
Confectioners' sugar or brown sugar

Combine 1 tablespoon of the sugar and the cinnamon, and set it aside. In a small skillet, melt 1 tablespoon of the butter over medium heat, add the apple slices, raisins and brandy, cider or juice. Sprinkle the cinnamon sugar into the pan, then cook and stir the apples for 3 to 4 minutes. Remove the mixture from the heat and drain it.

Preheat the oven to 425 degrees. Melt the remaining tablespoon of butter in a 10-inch ovenproof skillet and set it aside. In a deep, narrow mixing bowl, beat the eggs with an electric mixer on high speed until they are foamy. Gradually add the flour and milk, alternating between the two and beating on high speed until the mixture is well blended.

Add the remaining tablespoon of sugar and the salt and

continue beating the mixture for 3 minutes more. Pour the mixture into the buttered skillet and bake uncovered for 10 minutes.

Immediately spoon the drained fruit mixture into the center of the pancake. Return it to the oven and bake another 10 to 15 minutes, until it is puffed and golden. Sprinkle it with confectioners' sugar or brown sugar. Using two spatulas, remove the pancake to a heated platter or serve from the skillet. Cut the pancake into wedges and serve immediately. Makes 2 or 3 servings.

COLONIAL RINGS

5 packages (3 tablespoons plus one teaspoon)
    active dry yeast
⅔ cup sugar
½ cup (1 stick) unsalted butter
1 teaspoon salt
4 eggs
1¾ teaspoons vanilla extract
6 cups bread flour
1½ cups chopped walnuts
⅓ cup sliced almonds
½ cup candied fruits
3 cups golden raisins
¼ cup (4 tablespoons) butter, melted
1 tablespoon light corn syrup
2 cups confectioners' sugar

Preheat the oven to 375 degrees 10 minutes before the rings are ready to be baked.

Lightly butter three 9-inch round cake pans. Combine 1 cup of lukewarm water with the yeast and 1 teaspoon of sugar in a bowl, and set it aside.

Beat the remaining sugar, butter and salt until fluffy. Add the eggs, one at a time, beating well after each addition. Add the yeast mixture and 1½ teaspoons of the vanilla. Gradually add the bread flour, beating constantly. Beat the dough for 5 minutes, then let the dough rest for 20 minutes.

Mix the nuts, candied fruits and raisins into the dough. Cover the dough and let it rise in a warm place until it doubles in bulk. Punch the dough down and divide it into thirds. Roll out each third into a rectangle about 14 by 7 inches, then spread the dough with some melted butter and roll it up like a jelly roll. Carefully form the roll into a ring, pinching the ends together gently to connect them. Repeat with the other two portions.

Cover the rings and let them rise in a warm place until they have increased in bulk by about a third. Brush the rings with melted butter and bake them for 40 minutes.

Combine the corn syrup, 3 tablespoons of lukewarm water and the remaining ¼ teaspoon of vanilla. Add the confectioners' sugar, beating the mixture until it is smooth. Spread this icing over the rings while they are still warm. Makes three rings. Each ring serves 6.

CHOCO-PEANUT BUTTER COFFEE RING

CAKE

2 to 2½ cups all-purpose flour
1 package (2 teaspoons) active dry yeast
½ cup whole milk
¼ cup sugar
2 tablespoons butter
½ teaspoon salt
1 egg

FILLING

¼ cup peanut butter
¼ cup sugar
2 tablespoons butter
½ cup semisweet chocolate pieces, melted

Stir together 1 cup of the flour and the yeast in a large mixing bowl. In a saucepan, heat the milk, ¼ cup of the sugar, 2 tablespoons of butter and salt only until warm, between 115 and 120 degrees. Add this to the flour mixture and add the egg. Beat the mixture at low speed with an electric mixer for 30 seconds, scraping the bowl constantly. Then continue to beat it for 3 minutes at high speed.

Stir in as much of the remaining flour as you can mix in with a spoon. Turn the dough out onto a lightly floured surface and knead in enough of the remaining flour to produce a moderately soft dough that is smooth and elastic, from 3 to 5 minutes. Place in a greased bowl and turn once to coat the dough. Cover the dough and let it rise until it has doubled in bulk, 1¼ to 1½ hours. Punch it down and let it rest for 10 minutes. Roll it into a 22 × 9-inch rectangle. Grease a cookie sheet.

For the filling, stir together the peanut butter, sugar, butter and melted chocolate. Blend completely. Then spread the peanut butter mixture over the dough. Roll the dough up from the long side into a jelly roll shape. Place on the greased baking sheet, sealing the ends together to form a ring. Slash the dough two-thirds through to the center at 1-inch intervals.

Cover the dough and let it rise until it has nearly doubled in bulk, about 30 minutes. Preheat the oven to 350 degrees. Bake for 20 to 25 minutes, covering the cake with foil after 15 minutes. Makes one coffee ring.

PORTUGUESE PUDIM FLAN

1½ cups heavy cream
1½ cups whole milk
¾ cup sugar
6 egg yolks
2 teaspoons port
Flower blossoms (for garnish)

Preheat the oven to 350 degrees. In a heavy saucepan, warm the cream and milk over high heat until small bubbles appear around the edge. Remove the saucepan from the heat and set it aside.

In a smaller heavy saucepan or skillet, caramelize the sugar by stirring it over moderate heat until it melts and turns a light golden brown. Immediately pour the hot cream and milk in a thin stream into the caramel, stirring it constantly with a large spoon. Continue to stir it until the caramel has dissolved completely.

With a whisk, or a rotary or electric beater, beat the egg yolks until they are well blended. Then slowly pour the cream mixture into the yolks, stirring constantly. Stir in the port. Then strain the mixture through a fine sieve a little at a time into a dozen 4-ounce heatproof porcelain or glass molds or custard cups.

Set the molds in a large roasting pan on the middle rack of the oven and pour in enough boiling water to come halfway up the sides of the cups. Bake the flans for 40 minutes, or until a knife inserted in the center of the custard comes out clean. Cool the flans to room temperature, then refrigerate them for at least 3 hours.

To unmold the flans, run a sharp knife around the inside edge of each mold and dip the bottoms briefly in hot water. Wipe the molds dry, place a chilled serving plate upside down over each and, grasping each mold and plate together, invert quickly. Rap the plate on a table. The custard should slide out easily. You can garnish the pudim flan with a flower blossom, as the Portuguese do. Makes one dozen.

GREEK GALAKTOBOUREKO

6 cups whole milk
1 cup fine semolina
3½ tablespoons cornstarch
3 cups sugar
¼ teaspoon salt
6 eggs
1 teaspoon vanilla extract (optional)
1 tablespoon butter
12 sheets commercial filo dough, unrolled flat
    and covered with a damp towel
¾ cup (1½ sticks) butter, melted and kept hot
1 lemon or orange peel
2 tablespoons fine brandy or Cognac
    (optional)

A Constantinople coffee house

Bring the milk gradually to a boil in a heavy-bottomed 3-quart saucepan. Do not allow it to scorch. Meanwhile, sift the semolina, cornstarch, 1 cup of the sugar and salt together and gradually add the mixture to the boiling milk, stirring it constantly with a wooden spoon. Cook it slowly over medium heat until the mixture thickens and comes to a full boil, then remove it from the heat.

Beat the eggs at high speed in an electric mixer. Gradually add ½ cup of the sugar and continue beating until it is very thick and fluffy, about 10 minutes. Add the vanilla if used. Stirring constantly, add the eggs to the hot pudding. Partially cover the pan and allow it to cool.

Preheat the oven to 350 degrees. Butter a 9 × 12 × 3-inch baking pan and cover the bottom with seven sheets of filo, brushing butter generously between each and making sure a few sheets come up the pan sides. Pour the custard into the pan over the filo. Cover with the remaining five sheets, brushing butter between each and on the surface.

With the tip of a very sharp knife, score the top filo

sheets into squares or diamond shapes, being careful not to score as deeply as the custard. Bake on the center rack of the oven for 40 to 45 minutes, until the filo is crisp and golden and the custard is firm. Meanwhile, boil the remaining 1½ cups of sugar with 1 cup of water and the lemon or orange peel for 5 minutes. Add the brandy or cognac, if desired, and set aside.

Remove the galaktoboureko from the oven and set it on a cake rack. Spoon the hot syrup over it, particularly over the edges. Cool it thoroughly before cutting and serving it. Store it in the refrigerator. Makes 20 to 24 squares.

Glossary

HERE is a collection of terms that might turn up during your search for the perfect cup of coffee. Technical terms from coffee contracts have been omitted, along with those referring to aspects of preparation that have no bearing on your consumer choice. This listing should provide a quick reference in times of curiosity or uncertainty.

A

Abyssinian. Officially Ethiopian. *Arabica* coffee produced mainly in the provinces of Djimmah, Sidamo, Lekampti and Salo in western and southwestern Ethiopia from wild trees.

acidity. Desirable cup characteristic. When used by the coffee trade, it does not refer to a greater amount of actual acid but to coffee that is smooth and rich and has verve, snap, life and thinness. Also referred to as "wineyness."

Addis Ababa. The capital of Ethiopia and the chief interior coffee market.

Aden.   Chief seaport of Arabia. One of the principal ports of shipment for Arabian Mocha and Abyssinian coffees.

Ahuachapán.   Department of El Salvador that produces coffee.

Alajuela.   City and province in Costa Rica. Coffees grown in the district are characterized by fine flavor, rich body and sharp acidity.

Alta Verapaz.   Department in the mountains of northern Guatemala, producing a gray-blue bean coffee with a fine mellow flavor. Usually called Cobán after the department's capital.

Amatitlán.   Town on the Pacific slope of Guatemala in which there are many coffee plantations.

Angola.   West African country that produces *robusta* coffees known as Novo Redondo, Ambion, Ambriz, Encoge and Cazenga, as well as some *arabica.*

Angra dos Reis.   Brazilian coffee port on Iena Grande Bay 75 miles west of Rio de Janeiro.

Ankola.   Coffee produced in the district of Ankola, Sumatra, in Indonesia. Considered one of the world's finest.

Antigua.   A district of Guatemala just west of Guatemala City. Its fine coffees are characterized by bluish color, pleasant acidity, body and flavor.

Antioquia.   A department of Colombia in which Medellíns are produced.

Approved Coffee Measure.   Also known as ACM, this is the proper proportion of water to coffee whether 6 cups are being brewed or 600: Two level tablespoons of ground coffee to every 6 ounces of water.

Arabigo.   Coffee seed, different from bourbon, being a larger flat-type bean. Considered better quality, most suitable for higher altitudes.

Halfpenny token from the Mary Long Coffee House

Armenia. Market name and town in the department of Caldas in Colombia.

B

Bahia. Now most often called Salvador, a seaport of Brazil, capital of state of Bahia and port of shipment for certain low grades of Brazilian coffee known by this name.

bale. Term applied to a Mocha or Harar coffee package, containing one bale known as a half. A half weighs 80 kilos, or 176 pounds.

Barahona. Seaport on the southern coast of the Dominican Republic. The beans grown here are handsome and large, considered the best from the island republic.

Barranquilla. Port in Colombia near the mouth of the Magdalena River. The principal export point for the east coast of Colombia.

Belgian Congo. Now known as Zaire. An African country that produces washed *arabica* of various grades. Also produces Congo *robusta*, both washed and natural.

black beans. Dead coffee beans that have dropped from the trees before harvest.

black jack. Term applied to coffee beans that have turned black during the process of curing, in the hold of a vessel during transport or because of disease.

Blue Mountain. District on the island of Jamaica producing the finest coffee grown on the island. It makes a good appearing roast and pleasantly aromatic cup.

Boconó. Town in western Venezuela, giving its name to the coffees grown in the district. Considered a grade of Maracaibo, they are frequently used as fillers in blends.

Boengie. District of the island of Celebes in Indonesia that produces a small amount of coffee sold under the name. Fine coffees from this district rank among the leading Indonesians.

Bogotá. Capital of the South American republic of Colombia. Coffees grown in the district surrounding the capital are noted for their acidity, body and flavor.

Bold.   Classification of coffee bean by size—larger than medium but smaller than large or extra large. Also, a generic reference to size, as in "sufficiently bold."

Bourbon Santos.   Coffee grown in Brazil and originally obtained from the Mocha seed. Today's Bourbon is distinctly a Brazil plant, since no trees or seeds have been brought in from the original source in more than a century. The finest coffee raised in Brazil, Santos is a small, curly bean producing a drink that is smooth and palatable.

Boyacá.   Department in Colombia that produces coffee commercially to a small degree.

Brazil.   World's largest producer of coffee, turning out at times as much as half the total supply. Brazil coffees include growths of drastically different characteristics and values, so they are better known by their districts of origin than simply as "Brazils."

broca.   Spanish name for the dreaded coffee bean borer, or *Hemileia vastatrix*.

Bucaramanga.   Market name and town in the department of Santander in Colombia. Commercial coffees from here are good for blending. Fancy Bucaramangas are considered equal to old Sumatras.

Buenaventura.   Principal coffee seaport on the Pacific coast of Colombia.

bullhead.   Monstrosity in which the coffee bean develops to more than twice its normal size. This usually occurs when two beans grow together, and they usually break apart during roasting.

C

café bonifeur.   French West Indies term applying to coffee that has been thoroughly cleaned and polished. Named after the polishing machine in Guadeloupe.

cafe de panno.   Portuguese term for coffee picked "in the cloth." A cotton sheet is spread on the ground under the tree—the beans do not touch the ground.

cafe despolpado.   In Portuguese, washed coffee or pulped coffee.

cafeate. Local term used in Nicaragua for coffee with milk.

caffeine. An alkaloidal substance found in the coffee bean, coffee leaf, tea leaf, yerba maté, cacao bean. The caffeine content of green coffee averages 1.5 percent.

Caldas. Department in Colombia in which Armenia, Manizales and Caldas coffees are produced.

Cali. Market name and town in the department of Valle del Cauca in Colombia.

Capitania. Market name for a certain quality of coffee arriving at the port of Vitória, Brazil.

Caracas. Capital of Venezuela. Also a name for coffees grown in the area and shipped through the city and its port, La Guaira.

caracol. Separation of coffee consisting of peaberries selected from firsts and seconds.

caracolilo. Spanish name given to small peaberry coffee, and also to the most popular type of Dominican coffee.

carangola. Natural hybrid, found in the district of that name, in Minas Gerais, Brazil.

Cartagena. One of the principal coffee seaports on the Caribbean coast of Colombia.

Cartago. City and province in Costa Rica twelve miles east of the capital, San José. The district produces a high grade of coffee. Also a city in Colombia.

Cauca. Colombia river and department, the latter producing the Cauca and popyan coffees.

Ceará. State in northern Brazil that produces a small amount of good-quality coffee sufficient for home consumption.

Champerico. Small seaport on the Pacific coast of Guatemala from which considerable coffee is shipped.

Chapada. Mountain in Brazil's Mato Grosso and general term for tableland of mountainous country. Certain coffees shipped from Bahia are called Chapada.

cherry. Name applied to the ripe fruit of the coffee tree. The seeds, with coverings removed, become green coffee.

Chiapas.   Coffee-producing district in Mexico near the Guatemalan border. Coffees grown here resemble Guatemalans.

chicory.   Addition or filler in coffee made from the plant *Cichorium intybus.* The raw root is cut into slices, kiln dried, then roasted in the same manner as coffee.

Chuva.   Mountainous coffee-producing region in the western part of the Guatemalan department of Quezaltenango.

city roast.   Term used in New York City to indicate a medium dark roasted coffee. Not as dark as full city roast.

Coatepec.   Coffee-producing district in Veracruz, Mexico. Sometimes ranked with the world's finest growths, coffees from this district feature more acidity than those from Mexico's west coast, along with more tang and excellent flavor.

Cobán.   Capital of the central Guatemalan department of Alta Verapaz. Coffee grown in this mountainous region is a waxy, bluish bean, making a handsome roast, spicy and aromatic in the cup. A particularly good blender.

coffee.   The U.S. Department of Agriculture defines coffee as "the seed of cultivated varieties of *Coffea arabica, C. liberica,* and *C. robusta.*"

coffee fruit.   A gossamerlike skin covers a soft pulp sweetish to the taste. This pulp in turn encases the inner seal, called the parchment, which covers each seed, or bean, outside the tight-fitting "silver skin."

coffee grader.   Official licensed by the Coffee Exchange whose duty it is to grade coffee according to types recognized by the exchange.

Colombia.   Republic in northwestern South America that produces some of the finest coffees grown. Best known are Medellíns, Manizales, Armenias, Bogotás, Bucaramangas, Tolimas, Cúcutas, Girardots and Hondas.

cordilleras.   Spanish term for the Andes in Colombia, on the slopes of which the republic's finest coffees are grown.

Córdoba.   City in the state of Veracruz, Mexico, that produces coffee. Too neutral to form the basis of a blend, it can be used to balance the tang of other grades.

Costa Rica. Most southern of the five Central American republics, producing one of the finest coffees in the world. With heavy body and sharp acidity, they are best adapted for blending.

Creoule. Common variety of coffee from the island of Trinidad.

Cuba. Coffees from this island are of varying quality, with beans of medium size, light green and producing a uniform roast.

Cúcuta. Market name and town in the Colombian department of Norte de Santander. Coffee from this district is usually shipped through the port of Maracaibo, Venezuela, and classified among the Maracaibo types. It ranks with Méridas and fine-grown Boconós.

Cundinamarca. Department of Colombia in which Bogotá, some Girardot and some Honda coffees are produced.

Curitiba. Coffee trading center and capital of the state of Paraná in Brazil.

D

Dire Dawa. Trading center in Ethiopia for Harar coffee.

Djakarta. Trading center for Java coffee, formerly called Batavia. The capital of the new republic of Indonesia. Sometimes spelled Jakarta.

Dominican Republic. West Indian republic occupying the eastern two-thirds of the island of Hispaniola. Coffee produced here, named after the capital of Santo Domingo, is blue-green and makes a handsome roast. It sports a rich, fairly acidy flavor in the cup.

dry fermenting. Process used to ferment washed coffee without water.

dry roast. Roasting process in which no water is used to check the roast, the operator depending entirely on his cooling apparatus.

E

Ecuador.   South American republic that produces coffee of the *arabica* type. Classed among the mild coffees.

Ensacador.   Brazilian word meaning "coffee bagger."

Escuintila.   Capital of the department of the same name in Guatemala, the center of a coffee-producing section.

Espírito Santo.   State in Brazil, the capital of which is Vitória.

Ethiopian.   See Abyssinian.

excelso.   Comprehensive grade of Colombian coffee consisting of qualities corresponding to *supremo* and *extra* types. May include peaberries of those types.

F

fazenda.   Portuguese term used in Brazil for a coffee plantation.

fermenting.   A step in the preparation of ripe coffee. Consists of putting pulped coffee into tanks, with or without water. Process takes hours to days, according to altitude and temperature.

finca.   Spanish word for farm, commonly used to mean coffee plantation.

flatbean Santos.   A larger bean and without the curly characteristics generally associated with Bourbon Santos. Usually void of acid.

French roast.   Term applied to roasted coffee, meaning the bean is roasted long enough to bring the natural oil to the surface.

full city roast.   Term applied to coffee in New York, indicating a roast slightly heavier than a city roast. Beans are roasted to their full development.

futures.   Purchase or sale of coffee or other commodity contracts for delivery in the future. Contracts are bought and sold like stocks.

G

Girardot.   Market name and Magdalena River shipping port in Colombia's department of Cundinamarca.

glazing.   Synonymous with coating. Roasted coffees are sometimes glazed to preserve their natural flavor and aroma, or to meet the demand of certain classes of trade, especially in the southern United States.

groundy.   Earthy taste sometimes found in damaged coffees. Different from mustiness.

Guadeloupe.   Island in the French West Indies with Pointe-à-Pitre as its chief port and Bass-Terre as its capital. Produces coffee of excellent quality, almost all of which is shipped to France.

Guatemala.   Central American republic that produces a stylish coffee. Mountain-grown beans make a handsome roast and are full, heavy in body and excellently flavored in the cup. Coffees grown lower are light in the cup but still flavorful.

Guaxupé.   Town in the state of Minas Gerais in Brazil. Coffees shipped under this name are high grade, acidy and flavory.

Guayaquil.   Ecuador's first port, through which most of its coffees are shipped.

H

hacienda.   Spanish term for farm or ranch. In Venezuela, usually means coffee plantation.

Haiti.   West Indian republic with growing importance as coffee producer. Haitian coffee has a large bean and heavy body. A flavory coffee well adapted to blending.

Hamakua.   Coffee-growing district in Hawaii that produces a good-quality bean.

Harar.   City and province in Ethiopia. Coffee now known as Harar used to be sold as either Longberry

Mocha or Abyssinian longberry. It is exported through Djibouti or Aden.

harsh.   Term used to describe a certain coffee flavor. Rio and similar coffees are denoted as harsh.

hidy.   Description of coffee that smells like hides. Odor can actually come from contact with hides.

Hodeida.   Fortified Yemen seaport on the Red Sea. An important shipping point for Mocha coffee.

Honda.   Town in the department of Tolima, Colombia, and former market name for Colombia coffee, now a gathering place for Tolima coffees. Shipping port is La Dorado on the Magdalena River.

Honduras.   Republic on the Caribbean coast of Central America that produces a small, round, bluish-green coffee of fair quality.

Huatusco.   Town in the state of Veracruz, Mexico, that produces coffee fine in appearance and right behind Coatepec for acidity and blending qualities.

Hulla.   Department of Colombia in which Neiva and Girardot coffees are produced.

hulling.   Last step before milling in the preparation of washed coffee. Operation is done by machines that remove the parchment and silver skin.

husking.   Cleaning coffee beans that have been dried in the cherry. Coffee is said to be "in the husk" when the whole fruit is dried without water.

I

Ibagué.   Market name and town in the department of Tolima, Colombia.

imperfections.   Black beans, broken beans, shells, immatures, quakers, stones and pods—imperfections in the sample that affect the way a coffee is graded.

Italian roast.   Term applying to coffee roasted darker than French. Used extensively by Italians, but also by many other coffee-producing countries.

Ivory Coast. French West Africa produces some 2.5 million bags of coffee each year, nearly all of it *robusta* and 75 percent coming from the Ivory Coast. The bulk of the crop is shipped to France, yet a healthy market has developed in the United States to make its instant coffees.

J

Jalapa. City and district in Mexico adjoining celebrated Coatepec and producing some fine coffee sold as Jalapa. A stylish roaster but rather neutral in the cup.

Jamaica. Largest of the British West Indies, with Kingston as its capital and shipping port. Produces two distinct types of coffee. The highland is led by the famed Blue Mountain and by Prime Jamaica Washed. The lowland is used chiefly as a filler in blends.

Java. Island in Indonesia, with principal ports of Djakarta, Semarang and Surabaja. Only coffees of the *Coffea arabica* variety grown on this island can be labeled Java in the United States, though the island now grows *robusta* and *liberica* as well.

Jinotega. City and department in northwestern Nicaragua that produces some of the country's best coffees.

K

kafa. Ethiopian coffee that grows wild.

Kenya. Country in East Africa that produces a high grade of the *arabica* variety sold under the nation's name.

Kona. District on the west side of the island of Hawaii. A large, blue, flinty bean, Kona is mild in acidity and striking in flavor.

L

La Guaira. Seaport of the federal district of Caracas, Venezuela. All Caracas coffees are shipped from here.

La Libertad.   Department and seaport of El Salvador that produces some coffee

La Unión.   City and department of El Salvador that produces a certain amount of coffee.

Liberian.   *Coffea liberica*, a species that originated in Liberia, Africa. Formerly mixed to some extent with Bourbon Santos but considered to be of a low grade.

Londrina.   Leading market center and second largest coffee-growing area in Paraná, Brazil

Longberry Harar.   Grade of coffee produced in Ethiopia, falling between the all-long-bean and the inferior all-short-bean.

M

Macassar.   Seaport on the island of Celebes, Indonesia, through which coffee is shipped.

Madras.   Seaport and district in southern India that grows and ships Malabar coffees.

Magdalena.   Principal river in Colombia on which a considerable amount of coffee moves by steamer to port. Also a department that produces Santa Marta coffee.

Malabar.   Name given to the best coffees from India. A small, blue-green bean with strong flavor and deep color in the cup.

Mandheling.   Coffee produced in Mandheling district on west coast of Sumatra, one of the finest and highest-priced coffees in the world.

Mangalore.   Seaport on the west coast of southern India, through which a large proportion of the subcontinent's coffee is exported.

Manizales.   Market name and town in the department of Caldas, Colombia. Coffees grown here are similar to Medellíns in the cup but lack the heavy body and some of the flavor.

Maracaibo.   Port on Lake Maracaibo, Venezuela. Important shipping point for Cúcuta and Trujillo coffees grown in Colombia, Mérida, Táchira, and Tovar grown nearby in Venezuela.

Maringá. Town and marketing center in North Paraná, Brazil, and one of the largest coffee-producing areas.

Matagalpa. Coffee-growing district of Nicaragua that produces a large, handsome, blue, washed bean. Makes a fancy roast with plenty of acidity in the cup.

Mattari. Coffee-growing district of Arabia, producing one of the superior grades of Mocha.

mazagran. French name for a drink composed of cold coffee and seltzer water.

Mbuni. Unwashed, native-grown *arabica* coffee from East Africa.

Medellín. Capital city of the Colombian department of Antioquia and name given to one of the finest Colombian coffees. Medellíns are fancy, mountain grown and esteemed for their high quality. Light to dark green as beans, they make handsome roasters and give fine flavor and body in the cup.

Menado. Seaport and district on the island of Celebes, Indonesia. Coffee from this district commands high prices in Europe for its superior quality.

Mérida. District of Venezuela that gives its name to one of the best Maracaibo coffees. Méridas are sought for their delicate flavor.

Mexico. Republic between the United States and Central America that produces some of the most important blending coffees. The best known are Oaxaca, Córdoba, Coatepec, Jalapa, Pluma Oaxaca and Tapachulas. In the cup, Mexican coffees are rich in body, fine in acidity and wonderful in bouquet.

mild coffees. Term formerly used to indicate those free from the harsh Rio flavor but now used to describe coffees produced in countries other than Brazil.

Minas Gerais. State in Brazil that produces Rio coffee of a peculiar flavor.

Mocha. Formerly important coffee port on the Red Sea coast of Yemen but closed by a sand bar more than a century ago. Only coffees grown in Yemen are entitled to the trade name Mocha. Now shipped through the ports of Hodeida and Aden, the beans are small and irregular, olive green to pale yellow. In the cup, they exhibit a unique winey character, with heavy body and extraordinarily smooth flavor.

Murtha. Santos coffee said to provide the finest and smoothest cup in this variety.

musty. Flavor often found in coffee as a result of either overheating, lack of proper drying or aging. Mustiness is generally undesirable.

Mysore. State of southern India that produces a mountain-grown coffee marketed principally in England.

N

Nicaragua. Coffee-producing country in Central America. Its washed coffees—95 percent of the crop—are fine roasters with pleasant acidity in the cup.

Norte de Santander. Department of Colombia that produces Cúcuta and Ocaña coffees.

O

Oaxaca. Capital of the state of Oaxaca in Mexico. Coffee from here is valued because of its sharp acidity and excellent flavor.

Old Government Java. Name formerly applied to coffee grown on native estates in Java and Sumatra and stored by the Dutch government.

Orizaba. Capital of the state of Veracruz in Mexico that gives its name to coffee produced in the surrounding dis-

Leather threepenny token from the Chapter Coffee House in Paternoster Row

trict. With good cup quality, this coffee ranks next to Huatusco.

P

Padang.   Principal shipping port on the west coast of Sumatra. Only Ankola and Mandheling coffees are shipped through this port.

Palembang.   District and shipping port on the southeast coast of Sumatra. Only *robusta* coffees are shipped through here.

Paraná.   Largest coffee-producing state in Brazil. Located in the southern section of the country, with Curitiba as its capital and Paranaguá as its shipping port. Paranás are mild to strong in flavor, similar to Santos in the cup but not quite as good.

parchment.   Endocarp of the coffee fruit. It lies between the flesh and the silver skin, and is removed during the hulling process.

peaberry.   Rounded bean from an occasional coffee cherry that contains only one seed instead of the usual flat-sided pair. This is due to nondevelopment of one of the ovules, an abortion most common among *arabica* trees.

Preanger.   District on the island of Java that at one time produced the finest of the native growths. Coffee is no longer grown there.

Puerto Barrios.   Guatemala's largest port and most important coffee-exporting town. It is on the Caribbean coast.

Puerto Berrio.   Town on the Magdalena River in Colombia through which almost all Medellín coffees are shipped.

Puerto Limón.   Atlantic port of Costa Rica, important for exports of Costa Rican coffee.

Puerto Rico.   Island in the West Indies whose superior grades of coffee rank among the best known in the trade. The cup has a peculiar flavor similar to a washed Caracas but smoother.

pulping.   First step after picking in the preparation of coffee by the wet method. Machines rub away the outer skin with friction without crushing the beans.

Q

quakers.   Blighted and undeveloped coffee beans. A few quakers are not considered harmful to cup quality, but a number of them will have a negative impact.

R

Ribeirão Prêto.   Town and coffee district in the state of São Paulo, Brazil, that produces a flavorful coffee.

Rio de Janeiro.   A state of Brazil, as well as its most important city. Rios are used in the United States mostly by virtue of their low price, since they are harsh and pungent in the cup. They do, however, have a certain following in the South dating back to the earliest days of the packaged coffee industry.

Rio flavor.   Heavy and harsh taste characteristic of coffees grown in Brazil's state of Rio de Janeiro. Sometimes present even in fancy mild coffees.

Robusta.   *Robusta* coffee, a species discovered growing wild in the Congo by Emil Laurent in 1898. A Belgian horticultural firm picked it up and gave it the generic name *robusta.* Though the cup quality is inferior to that of *arabica* coffees, the tree is far more hardy—giving it a certain desirability to growers. Now cultivated extensively in Indonesia.

Rubiaceae.   Botanical family to which coffee belongs.

S

Salvador, El.   Central American republic producing a medium bean, fair-roasting coffee. The high grown are of full body and good quality. The United States takes most of El Salvador's coffee.

Sanani. Mocha coffee from the Sana region of Yemen. One of the better grades of Mochas, though seldom seen in the United States.

San José. The most important port on the Pacific coast of Guatemala. Also, the capital of Costa Rica and the principal marketing center for that republic's coffees.

Santa Marta. Market name and Atlantic port in the department of Magdalena, Colombia. Now Colombia's largest Atlantic port.

Santander. Department of Colombia that produces Bucaramanga coffee.

Santos. Principal shipping port for coffee in Brazil, 200 miles southwest of Rio de Janeiro and 49 miles from São Paulo. The city gives its name to coffee passing through it. These have the general distinction of being the best grown in Brazil.

São Paulo. State, with capital city of the same name, in Brazil. One of the world's largest and richest coffee areas, producing almost a third of all Brazilian coffees.

Semarang. Seaport town on the north coast of Java. Coffee sold by this name is a small, yellowish green bean that brews light and thin in the cup.

Shortberry Harar. The shortest bean Harar coffee.

Sibolga. Coffee shipping port on the west coast of Sumatra. Ankola coffees are shipped through this port.

silver skin. The thin, papery covering on the surface of the coffee bean, inside the parchment.

sizing. Grading green coffee beans by size. Usually done by machines that separate and distribute the different beans. The principal grades are triage, third flats, second flats, first flats, and first and second peaberries.

Soconusco. Large coffee district in the Mexican state of Chiapas near the Guatemalan border.

sorting. The use of electronic color-sensitive machinery to eliminate all beans lighter or darker than a standard to obtain coffee of top quality.

spot.   The opposite of futures. Importers, brokers, jobbers and roasters deal in actual coffee in warehouses or in consuming countries.

style.   A grade term used to designate the appearance of a whole coffee bean, either green or roasted.

Sumatra.   Island of Indonesia. Included among Sumatran coffees are several ranked among the finest in the world. Mandheling and Ankola are the best known.

summer roast.   Roasters frequently give beans a lighter roast in summer than in winter to prevent sweating caused by the season's heat.

supremo.   Top grade of Colombian coffee.

sweet.   Trade term used to describe coffee free from the harshness associated with Rio and also from any form of damage.

T

Tabasco.   Small coffee-producing state in Mexico on the Gulf of Mexico.

Táchira.   Coffee-producing state in western Venezuela. Until recent years, Táchira coffee was sold as Cúcuta. Now it is shipped under the name Táchira-Venezuela, while Cúcuta is marked Cúcuta-Colombia.

Tanzania.   East African country that produces an *arabica* coffee known as Tanganyika and a *robusta* named Bukoba.

tannin.   Tannic acid, a solid, yellowish white, astringent compound. The tannin content of green coffee averages 8 percent, with roasting cutting that by about half.

Tellicherry.   Port on the west coast of southern India, ranking right under Mangalore in coffee shipments. The district of Tellicherry produces a good grade of coffee.

Telok-Betong.   Coffee shipping port on the southeast coast of Sumatra. *Robusta* coffees from the district of Lampong are shipped through this port.

Timor. Principal island of the Timor Archipelago, east of the Sunda Islands and north of Australia. The northern section, a Portuguese possession, produces a certain amount of good-quality coffee known as Timor. It is shipped through the port of Dilly.

tipping. Charring the little germ at the end of the coffee bean by applying intense heat too quickly during the roasting process.

Tolima. Department of Colombia that produces Tolima, Ibagué, Libano, some Girardot and some Honda coffee.

Tovar. Town in Venezuela producing coffee with fair to good body but a duller roast than Cúcutas. Used for blending with Bourbon Santos.

Tres Ríos. Village and important district in Costa Rica, producing some of the finest coffee grown. The village is six miles from the capital of San José.

triage. French term used by the coffee trade of some countries to describe broken beans. Or, method of process used to limited degree in Haiti.

Turkish coffee. A reference to a flourlike grind on a dark roast, or to preparation in a style favored in the Middle East.

U

Uganda. Country in East Africa producing coffee generally marketed under that name.

unwashed coffee. Green coffee developed by the dry process, drying the entire fruit and removing parchment and silver skin by hulling operations.

Uruapan. City in the state of Michoacan, Mexico, that produces a famous coffee, although not in commercial quantities.

Uslutan. Leading coffee-producing department in El Salvador.

V

Valle de Cauca.   Department in Colombia in which Valle, Cali and Sevilla coffees are grown.

Venezuela.   Country in the northwest section of South America producing coffees in large volume and a wide variety of types. Some of the better known are Maracaibo, Caracas, Mérida and Táchira.

Victoria.   Former name of Vitória, a coffee port in the Brazilian state of Espírito Santo; also a type of coffee bean. Ranking fourth among Brazilian coffees, Victorias are large, dingy green or brown beans that make a roast free of quakers but muddy in the cup.

W

washed coffee.   Coffee that has been pulped, fermented, washed, dried and hulled. The ripe fruit is passed through a pulper that takes off the outer skin. The gummy substance is removed by fermentation and washing, with drying, hulling and separating to complete the preparation process.

W.I.P.   West Indian Preparation, a reference to coffee washed on the plantation.

Y

Yemen.   Section of old Arabia along the Red Sea, famous for producing a superior grade of coffee denoted Mocha.

A Coffee Reference List

SOME readers in search of additional information on specific aspects of coffee, or simply a different view of things, should search out the following books. A few remain readily available in book shops, while the rest can be found in many public libraries. Books in the first category will be helpful to the new coffee gourmet who seeks a deeper understanding of his chosen avocation. Those in the second group offer wide-ranging information on production and marketing, and the periodicals deliver regular updates to the international body of coffee knowledge.

GENERAL INFORMATION

Anderson, Kenneth. *The Pocket Guide to Coffees and Teas.* New York: G. P. Putnam and Sons, 1982.
Bramah, Edward. *Tea and Coffee.* London: Hutchinson, 1972.
Davids, Kenneth. *Coffee: A Guide to Buying, Brewing and Enjoying.* Revised. San Francisco: 101 Productions, 1981.

233

Dyer, Ceil. *Coffee Cookery*. Tucson, Arizona: Fisher Publishing, 1978.

Jacob, Heinrick Eduard. *Coffee: The Epic of a Commodity*. New York: Viking Press, 1935

Quimme, Peter. *The Signet Book of Coffee and Tea*. New York: Signet Classic Paperbacks, 1976.

Schafer, Charles and Violet. *Coffee: A Connoisseur's View*. San Francisco: Random House, Yerba Buena Press, 1976.

TECHNICAL INFORMATION

Haarer, A. E. *Modern Coffee Production*. 2d ed. London: Leonard Hill Ltd., 1962.

McKaye. *The Coffeeman's Manual*. New York: The Spice Mill Publishing Co., 1942.

Quinn, James. *Scientific Marketing of Coffee*. Whitestone, New York: The Tea and Coffee Trade Journal, 1960.

Schapira, Joel, David and Karl. *The Book of Tea and Coffee*. New York: St. Martin's Press, 1975.

Sivetz, Michael. *Coffee*. Corvallis, Oregon: Coffee Publications, 1977.

―――. *Coffee Technology*. New York: AVI Publications, 1977.

Ukers, William H. *All About Coffee*. 2d ed. Whitestone, New York: The Tea and Coffee Trade Journal, 1935.

PERIODICALS

American Automatic Merchandiser. Harcourt Brace Jovanovich, New York. Monthly.

Coffee Annual. George Gordon Paton and Co., New York. Annually.

Complete Coffee Coverage. George Gordon Paton and Co., New York. Daily.

National Coffee Association of the USA Newsletter. National Coffee Association, New York. Weekly.

Tea and Coffee Trade Journal. Tea and Coffee Trade Journal Co., Whitestone, New York. Monthly.

Vending Times. Vending Times Inc., New York. Monthly.

What's Brewing. National Coffee Service Association, Washington, D.C. Six times annually.

World Coffee & Tea. McKeand Publications, West Haven, Connecticut. Monthly.

INDEX

International Coffee Organization, Library Monthly Indexes. International Coffee Organization, London. Monthly, including an annual index.

Index